love
& war

ALSO BY JOHN ELDREDGE

Fathered by God: Learning What Your Dad Could Never Teach You
Walking with God: Talk to Him. Hear Him. Really.
Way of the Wild Heart: A Map for the Masculine Journey
Captivating: Unveiling the Mystery of a Woman's Soul
  (with Stasi Eldredge)
Epic: The Story God Is Telling
Waking the Dead: The Glory of a Heart Fully Alive
Wild at Heart: Discovering the Secret of a Man's Soul
Desire: The Journey We Must Take to Find the Life God Offers
The Sacred Romance (with Brent Curtis)

Finding the Marriage
You've Dreamed Of

love

&

war

JOHN AND STASI ELDREDGE

DOUBLEDAY RELIGION
New York London Toronto Sydney Auckland

ⅅⅅ
DOUBLEDAY

Copyright © 2009 by John Eldredge and Stasi Eldredge

All rights reserved.
Published in the United States by Doubleday Religion, an imprint of the Crown
Publishing Group, a division of Random House, Inc., New York. Published in associa-
tion with Yates & Yates, www.yates2.com.
www.crownpublishing.com

Doubleday and the DD colophon are registered trademarks of Random House, Inc.

Library of Congress Cataloging-in-Publication Data
Eldredge, John, 1960–
   Love & war : finding the marriage you've dreamed of / John and Stasi Eldredge. —
1st ed.
      p. cm.
   ISBN 978-0-385-52980-8
   1. Marriage—Religious aspects—Christianity.   I. Eldredge, Stasi.   II. Title.
   BV835.E38 2009
   248.8'44—dc22

                                                                        2009021286

ISBN 978-0-385-52980-8

Printed in the United States of America

10 9 8 7 6 5 4 3 2 1

First Edition

For Sam, Blaine, and Luke—and your future wives!
Because we love you more than we can say. And we have a strong
hunch that one day each of you will marry. So here's to you and the
woman you will pledge your life to. Here's to an everlasting love.

CONTENTS

Acknowledgments   xi

Introduction: It Can Be Done   1

1   Remembering What We Wanted   9

2   Love and War   23

3   A Perfect Storm   40

4   The Greatest Gift You Can Give   57

5   More Than Just Roommates   73

6   How to Have a Really Good Fight   88

7   A Shared Adventure   107

8   Back-to-Back with Swords Drawn   125

9   The Little Foxes   141

10 When Storms Descend   157

11 The Chapter on Sex   175

12 Learning to Love   192

Epilogue   210

Appendix: Prayers   212

ACKNOWLEDGMENTS

Our thanks are due to many, far too many to mention here. We have learned so much from friends, family, pastors, authors, and teachers. We have witnessed many marriages and taken careful notes. Many of you have played a role in helping to rescue our marriage. To all of you, past and present, who have poured into our lives, we thank you. But we would be remiss to not mention a few folks by name. Craig and Lori, your commitment to grow in loving each other well is inspiring. Thank you for inviting us as newlyweds into your marriage group. Thank you for living and loving so well. Thanks to our editor, Ken Petersen, and our new friends at Random House. Curtis and Sealy, thank you for your amazing work, loyal friendship, and unending support.

And to the King of Kings, our Lord Jesus Christ, who is our life, our breath, our truest Love, may you be pleased and blessed, and use this little book for your glory.

love
&
war

It Can Be Done

"Dearly Beloved, we have gathered here today in the presence of God to witness the joining together of this man and this woman in Holy Matrimony. The bond and covenant of marriage was established by God in creation, and our Lord Jesus Christ adorned this manner of life by his presence and first miracle at a wedding in Cana of Galilee. . . ."

And so the ceremony begins.

It is a ritual ancient as time and young as the hearts of the man and woman standing before us. (These brides and grooms look younger every year.) John is officiating. The bride and groom are dear friends. They are in love. We, their family and friends, are here to support them, celebrate them, all dressed up in our Sunday best. The church is glowing with candlelight; the flowers are so lovely. The groom looks terrified but happy; the bride is nervous and radiant. Suddenly I wonder, *Did I sit on the proper side? Was it bride's side on the left, groom's side on the right? Or the other way around?* The brides-maids are stunning. *Oh dear. They won't be wearing those dresses ever again!*

John continues, "The union of husband and wife in heart, body, and mind is intended by God for their mutual joy. . . ."

He looks so handsome in a suit and tie. I remember how he

1

looked on our wedding day in that fabulous black tux with tails. *I hope he asks me to dance at the reception.*

"Therefore marriage is not to be entered into unadvisedly or lightly, but reverently, deliberately, and in accordance with the purposes for which it was instituted by God."

The liturgy begins to settle us in. The church quiets, the coughing subsides, people are paying attention.

"Who gives this woman to be married to this man?"

No matter how many weddings I attend, there is something inexplicably stirring about all this—the ceremony, the making of vows, the great cloud of witnesses, something about this remarkable act feels—how does one describe it? Mythic.

"Daniel and Megan, you are about to abandon yourselves to each other, throw caution to the wind, forsake independence, isolation, and all others. You will vow to each other your undying love. Before you do, we must call this what it is—this is perfect madness."

That got the crowd's attention.

"As an aspiration, how lovely. As a reality, how rare. Everyone wants love; everyone is looking for love. Few seem to find what they are looking for; fewer still seem able to sustain it. Why in heaven's name would you come to church to publicly dedicate yourselves to something so risky, so fraught with danger, so *scandalous*? 'The heart has its reasons,' Pascal confessed, 'that reason knows not of.' Deep in the wellspring of our hearts there is a desire—for intimacy, beauty, and adventure. And no matter what anyone might say, we look for it all the days of our lives.

"Friends, I know what you are thinking. As you watch this today, there is something in your heart that says, 'Well, maybe. Maybe this time. Maybe this couple.' But what if, what if Daniel and Megan, in all their frail humanity, are living out before us right now a picture, a metaphor of something far more real and substantial. I'd like to suggest that this is no common passion play. Things are never what they seem. If you would see things clearly you must see with the eyes of the heart. That is the secret of every fairy tale, because it is the secret to the Gospel, because it is the secret to life.

"Scripture tells us that we might at any time entertain an angel simply by welcoming a stranger. The serpent in the garden is really the Prince of Darkness. The carpenter from Nazareth—there is more to him than meets the eye as well. Things are not what they seem, and so if we would understand our lives—and especially our marriages—we must listen again to the Gospel and the fairy tales based upon it. There are larger events unfolding around us, events of enormous consequence. A lamp is lit and love is lost. A box is opened and evil swarms into the world. An apple is taken and mankind is plunged into darkness. Moments of immense consequence are taking place all around us. Especially this.

"Dearly Beloved, you see before you a man and a woman. But there is more here than meets the eye. God gave to us this passion play to reenact, right here and now, the story of the ages. This is the story of mankind, the one story we have been telling ourselves over and over again, in every great myth and legend and poem and song. It is a love story, set in the midst of desperate times, set in the midst of war. It is a story of a shared quest. It is a story of romance. Daniel and Megan are playing out before you now the deepest and most mythic reality in the world. This is the story of God's romance with mankind."

I'm curious what the audience is thinking. When John speaks of love and marriage as deeper than fairy tale, what does our heart say in reply? I know the young women listening just said in their hearts, *Oh I hope that is true! I long for that to be true!* The young men are wondering, *If that is true, what is this going to require of me?* The older women filter this through the years of our actual marital experience; they are thinking, *Hmmm.* (It is a mixture of *Yes, I once longed for that,* and, *Perhaps it will come true for her; I wonder if it still might come true for me.*) And the older men sitting here now are simply thinking, *I wonder if the reception will have an open bar.*

"You don't believe me," John says. "But that's because we don't understand fairy tales and we don't understand the Gospel which they are trying to remind us of. They are stories of danger; they are stories where evil is very, very real. They are stories which require immense courage and sacrifice. A boy and a girl thrown together in some desperate journey. If we believed it, if we actually saw what was taking place right here, right now, we would cross ourselves. We would say desperate prayers, earnest prayers. We would salute them both and we would hold our breath for what happens next. Daniel and Megan, it is time to make your vows. After this, there is no turning back."

I find myself wondering, *What did the ancients know, that they placed vows at the core of this ceremony?* Did they understand that the crushing weight of all our desire would break a marriage, that we needed something far more substantial to secure this frail union? It makes me think of the Special Forces, vowing their lives to one another as they embark on a perilous mission in dark lands, the outcome of which remains quite uncertain. Vows.

". . . from this day forward, for better, for worse, for richer, for poorer, in sickness and in health, to have and to hold, to love and to cherish, till death do us part, according to God's holy ordinance, and forsaking all others, I will be yours alone as long as we both shall live."

The church is now very, very quiet. Only the older couples have any idea what these lovebirds have just promised, bless their hearts. They really believe that their marriage will somehow avert the darker side of the pledge; surely what they have in mind now is all their hopes and dreams of the "for better, richer, in health" parts. We all believed that. But Cortés has just burned his ships, and a good thing, too.

Next comes the rings, and John's charge to the couple. I love this part. What do you say to the young man entering marriage? What do you say to the young woman?

"Daniel, you are about to give your life away. You are stepping up, you are volunteering for the toughest assignment a man will ever be given: to offer your heart and your strength to Megan, time and time and time again, for the rest of your days. You have some sense of the weightiness of it. That's why you have that nervous grin on your face. But there was a reason they chose young men to send to the beaches at Normandy; they did not for the most part know what was coming. Older men would have been harder to recruit. I will not lie to you—nothing will be harder. And nothing will be richer. My words to you today are: It can be done. And it is worth it. To discover that because of your strength and your sacrifice Megan can become the woman she was meant to be, that somehow your fierce love can free her heart and release her beauty—that is worth whatever this may cost you. By the grace of God, you can do this. You have what it takes.

"Megan, you have dreamed of this day for a long, long time. And now you, also, are about to give your life away. It might seem easy and natural at first, to offer your feminine heart and your vulnerable beauty to Daniel. But do not be deceived. Nothing requires more courage than for a woman to truly offer herself to her man time and time and time again. Look around. Do you see many older women risking this? But I also say to you: It can be done. And it is worth it. To discover that because of your beauty and your sacrifice Daniel can become the man he was meant to be, that somehow your fierce love can free his heart and arouse his strength—that is worth whatever this may cost you. By the grace of God, you can do this. You are that beautiful woman.

"Daniel, Megan, in choosing marriage you have chosen an assignment at the frontlines in this epic battle for the human heart. You will face hardship, you will face suffering, you will face opposition, and you will face a lie. The scariest thing a woman ever offers is to believe that she is worth pursuing, to open her heart up to pursuit, to continue to open up her heart and offer the beauty she holds inside, all the while fearing it will not be enough. The scariest thing a man ever chooses is to offer his strength without knowing how things will turn out. To take the risk of playing the man before the outcome is decided. To offer his heart of strength while fearing it will not be enough.

"A lie is going to come to both of you, starting very soon, in subtle and not-so-subtle ways. It can't be done. It's too hard. We had unrealistic expectations. It isn't worth it. The lie to you, Megan, will be, 'You are nothing more than a disappointment.' And the lie to you, Daniel, will be, 'You are not really man enough for this.' And so, I have two words for you today. Words that I want you to keep close in your hearts as you go forward: You are. Megan, you are radiant, you shimmer, you shine, you are a treasure of a woman, a gem, you are. Daniel, you are a man, you are strong, and you are valiant. You have what it takes. Hold this close to your hearts. It can be done. And it is worth it."

John pauses to let this all sink in. I know what he is doing—he is speaking to *us,* to the men and women watching, far more than to dear Daniel and Megan who are too excited, and weary, filled with adrenaline and hormones and somewhat delirious by this point that they will only remember these words if they watch the tape later. Like premarital counseling, so much of the wisdom of this moment cannot be appreciated until we have a few years of "life together" under our belts. Then we have ears to hear. So John pauses for us to take it all in. A breeze blows through the sanctuary. The candles flicker in reply with a higher flame. I hope that is what is happening in every heart. May the fire within each of our hearts leap to the hope of this message.

And then he prays. We *need* to pray by this point; we have been practically holding our breath. We need a release for the tension and somewhere deep in our souls we know help is needed from higher places.

"Father, we believe in you. We believe you are God, the creator of life and love and the only one who makes it all possible. We come to you, more desperate than we know, to ask your Presence here, your favor upon Daniel and Megan, to ask your deepest blessing upon their marriage. Give them courage. Give them a clear heart and mind and will for all that they have just now pledged. And give to us, their witnesses, eyes to see and ears to hear what you are saying to each of us, through this passion play. Let hope arise. Let love prevail. In the name of Jesus Christ, our Lord. Amen."

Then comes the kiss (*okay, maybe I love this part the most, it's so romantic*). And the presentation of the new couple. Cheers. Music. Somewhere in the heavens, I imagine trumpets sounding and white doves being released. How God must love this!

As we join the recessional and walk out of the church into the warm summer evening, we are all caught up for a moment in a joyful sobriety. The timeless ritual, the courage and love of the young couple, and the deeper mythic story are having an effect upon us. As well they should. Desire is stirring within us. Longing calls to us. This is what we all were made for.

A warm breeze swirls among the crowd, and we instinctively turn our faces into it. The exotic perfume of magnolia and jasmine are in the air, mingling with the music coming from the reception party. The words linger in our midst. Even the older couples sense the beckoning. John and I are holding hands. I notice that a number of the couples are holding hands. It can be done. And it is worth it. Of all the things a man or woman needs to hear about marriage, this is perhaps the most important of all.

It can be done.

And it is worth it.

ONE

Remembering What We Wanted

See! The winter is past, the rains are over and gone. Flowers appear on the earth; the season of singing has come. . . . Arise, come, my darling; my beautiful one, come with me.

—SONG OF SONGS 2:11–13

Where do you pick up the story of a marriage? With the first kiss? (It was intoxicating.) The late-night phone calls? (They went on for hours.) With an evening picnic on the beach? (It was romantic.) Getting caught by a college roommate making out? (Now that was embarrassing.) When is that moment you decide, *I want to be with this person for the rest of my life?*

Maybe the best place to pick up this story is two years after "I Do," when we are talking divorce.

It was a Sunday. John and I were sitting at our hand-me-down card table having breakfast, in a tiny little matchbox of a house we rented. It was a pretty spring morning in southern California. The hydrangeas were blooming pink and blue on our front porch. I remember the sun filtering through the windows; a beam of light falling across the table between us. But it felt like a wall of glass. I was on my side, John was way over there. It was only a foot or so, but he felt miles away to me. Again.

The day was fresh but I was tired. Tired of trying. Tired of feeling like an utter disappointment to my husband who not that many months ago had pledged his heart to me for life. In front of everybody, I might add. Did he even mean it? It wasn't working. Our marriage wasn't anywhere near what I had imagined it would be.

I broke the familiar silence. "Maybe we should just get a divorce."

We had been married less than three years; our marriage had been full of promise, hope, and possibility. Heavens, I had known the man for five years before we even started dating, and we dated for three years before getting married. We were bright and rising stars. John worked on the staff of a church; I was working for a Christian ministry reaching out to troubled teens. Everyone thought we were the ideal couple.

How did we wind up here? What had gone so terribly wrong?

At the time, I would have said that I was utterly lonely—and to be lonely in your marriage is the loneliest feeling on earth. John was busy with his life and getting busier every day. It was a good life; he was involved in good things. The problem was, I didn't feel a part of it. I felt unnecessary to him. I, too, was working full-time, putting him through college. I came home to a man who was too tired to hear about my day, my world, all the dramas of the workplace. And I was too tired to care much about his. Sure, I would type his papers— but what happened to the shared vision? The desire to live life *together*? Two being better than one and all that?

I knew John was no longer smitten by me. I wondered if he even saw me. Almost as soon as we said our vows, I began to overeat. Within a few months of our wedding, I had put on twenty-five pounds. Something was up; something was broken. I needed comfort and relief and I turned to the drive-thru to find it. Packing on the weight sent a message to John that was clear and strong: *I am leaving you. You are not worth being beautiful for.*

And the weight continued to pile on. Diets began. I lost weight. I gained more. I lost weight. I gained more. Many of you know this dreadful cycle. Finally, seventy pounds heavier and almost three years married, I was desperate. A good friend had had success losing lots of weight through a medical fast, so I tried that. I stuck to it with perseverance and determination, hoping that once the weight was off, our marriage would heal and become everything I longed for it to be. At the end of the program I weighed twenty pounds less than when we got married. Ta-da!

It didn't help.

My suggestion of divorce came up months after finishing the fast.

What We Now Understand

Looking back, I see what a broken young woman I was—a little girl, really, longing to be loved and nearly certain I never would be. I didn't deserve to be loved. When I was young I just wanted someone to delight in me, but it never happened. I wasn't seen, and I wasn't wanted.

I brought that wounded heart into my marriage. *Hurrah, John—you get to be the one to delight in me and love me and fill this broken heart.* But even when John *did* love me, I didn't believe him. There was always a part of me waiting for the other shoe to drop. All my friendships growing up were tales of betrayal and abandonment, including every boyfriend before John. I was just waiting, believing I was a deep disappointment, and when you walk around like that, you are afraid all the time.

I see now how I looked to John to fill me. When he didn't come through, I blamed myself. I turned to food because I didn't know how to handle the hunger and disappointment in my heart.

Let me [John here] tell you what was going on for me that Sunday morning when Stasi brought up divorce. *Divorce.* I was a deer in the headlights. The word caught me completely by surprise.

What!? Where did this come from? Did she just say "divorce"? Something in me panicked. Alarms started going off. But had you asked me for my take on the suggestion, "Maybe we should get a divorce," I think at the time I would have said, *What is she talking about? I'm a great guy. We have a great marriage. This has to be about her. She's asking too much. She's looking to me to be everything.*

I'm embarrassed to admit that had you pressed me right then and there at the kitchen table, I don't think I could have named one issue on my part that played into Stasi's unhappiness. I was bewildered (something men seem to have a unique proficiency for). I found myself wondering, *How did we get here? When did this happen?*

But looking back now, I see what was going on. (Hindsight is 20/20, as the saying goes.) I entered marriage a frightened boy in a young man's body. A confusing mixture of self-centeredness (*Stasi, you lucky girl, you get to marry me!*) and vast insecurity (*I don't know if I can handle this.*). I had been so hurt by wounds I received in my youth and in previous relationships that I'd come to believe love never really lasted. So I had made a vow, years before, forgotten but still unyielding, that *I would never need anybody.* That vow became a source of lasting sorrow in our marriage.

There is a settled assurance a man comes to possess when he knows he is a man, and it enables him to enter his world with courage and kindness. The experience could not have been more foreign to me. I was scared. So, I faked it. I played the part of the great guy. I put on an air of bravado, like a boy wearing Superman pajamas. I overcompensated for my fears and landed in perfectionism. I became a driven, demanding overachiever with a generous dose of narcissism. Now, perfectionism is something you want in your tax attorney or your oncologist, but it is a horrible thing to be married to.

To be fair, a man needs to feel like a success, wants to feel like, "I have what it takes." He wants others to agree—especially his wife. I found myself in a marriage I didn't know squat about, with an alive and loving and broken woman, and I knew I was in *way* over my head. I didn't know anything about how to love a woman. I didn't know how to deal with her brokenness or mine. I was twenty-three. I was as ready for marriage as I was to take up the presidency. And so, I did what most men do—I ran. To work.

I was leading a small theater company at the time, and frankly, I was fabulous. A natural. I could write, act, and direct. I understood set design and construction. I shimmered; I was in my glory. Theater was my passion, my gifting, my calling. What makes the story messy is that it became my *mistress*. I began to spend more and more time at work, giving *it* the best of me, and all the while withdrawing from my wife. It was nothing short of an affair, but worse for the fact that it couldn't be so easily named. Folks thought I was amazing. I believed them.

It was a disaster waiting to happen.

This should have been our announcement in the Sunday paper wedding column:

> *Will Anyone Ever Love Me? was joined in marriage to I Will Never Need Anyone last week. The groom, Mr. Insecure Perfectionist, wedded his bride Miss I Know I'm a Disappointment at the Congregational Church. The lovely train wreck has taken up residence in Monrovia. A public reception and private disaster are soon to follow.*

What made our story confusing—and delayed our breakthrough— was the fact that we were really involved at church. We had gone through premarital counseling. We had read a few marriage books (okay, maybe just one). Someone had kindly given us one of those marriage weekend seminars in our first year (did they see something?) and we'd gone, enjoyed it, aced all the exercises. We were in a weekly married couples group, for heaven's sake! We had all the tips and techniques.

But those tools apparently missed the issues of the heart. Like rearranging deck chairs on the *Titanic*.

Romance Meets Reality

Maybe we ought to just start this book here: Marriage is fabulously hard.

Everybody who has been married knows this. Though years into marriage it still catches us off guard, all of us. And newly married couples, when they discover how hard it is, they seem genuinely surprised. Shocked, and disheartened, by the fact. *Are we doing something wrong? Did I marry the right person?* The sirens that lure us into marriage—romance, love, passion, sex, longing, companionship— seem so far from the actual reality of married life we fear we have made a colossal mistake, caught the wrong bus, missed our flight. And so the hardness also comes as something of an embarrassment. (Don't you feel embarrassed to admit how hard your marriage is?) *Maybe it's just us.*

Nope. This is everyone. We might as well come out and say it.

The sooner we get the shame and confusion off our backs, the sooner we will find our way through. Of course marriage is hard. For heaven's sake, bring together a man and a woman—two creatures who think, act, and feel so differently you would think they'd come from separate solar systems—and ask them to get along for the rest of their lives under the same roof. That is like taking Cinderella and Huck Finn, tossing them in a submarine, and closing the hatch. What did you think would happen?

Now, while you are at it, toss into that constantly-in-your-face experience all our fears, our wounded hearts, our self-centeredness, our self-doubt, and our resolute commitment to self-protection. Good Lord. Anyone looking for undeniable proof in the existence of God need look no further—the fact that *any* marriage makes it is a miracle of the first order. Bona fide proof that there are forces in the universe working on behalf of mankind.

All those fairy tales about a boy and girl who find themselves thrown together into an adventure in a dangerous land, and how they must come to work together if they have any hope of making it through, but they are both carrying a tragic flaw, an Achilles' heel that pricks the other constantly and they barely *do* make it through— those fairy tales pretty much have it right.

In fact, if you look back at the first marriage, that almost fairy-tale-like story in Genesis, you will see that Adam and Eve had a pretty rough go at it. And they didn't even have parents to screw them up as children or friends giving them ridiculous advice. My goodness, the Fall of man seems to come during the honeymoon, or shortly thereafter. (And how many honeymoon stories reenact that little drama?) They hit rough water as soon as they set sail, poor things. If this is the story of the first marriage, it is a bit sobering.

But it also gives us some encouragement, too. It is normal for marriage to be hard. Even the best of marriages.

I [John] wish some older man had pulled me aside a few weeks before our wedding, and said,

Now listen, son. You're a fine young man; Stasi is a wonderful girl. I think you two are made for each other. I'm very excited about this marriage. But now listen to me, lad—are you paying attention? You are also, both of you, deeply broken people. And all that brokenness is going to start coming to the surface as soon as you say, "I do." Don't let this throw you. It happens to everyone. It doesn't mean you've done something wrong. But what would *be wrong would be to ignore what surfaces. God is going to use your marriage to get to issues in your life he wants to address. You've got a way of making life work, and you're going to discover that Stasi does, too. That's all going to collide sooner or later. You might make it a year or two on young love, and thank God for it. But don't ignore this stuff when the fairy tale hits the fan. Get some help.*

Very few of us ever receive—or listen to—this kind of counsel, even years into our marriage. Things become hard; we are at first surprised, then dismayed. Eventually, if the situation doesn't improve, we fall into resignation. We check out, we disappear—emotionally, mentally, sometimes physically. He watches television all weekend; she eats or goes shopping.

I was trying to think of a good operating definition of marriage the other day and this is what I came up with: *Two guarded people managing their disappointment, negotiating for better terms through a DMZ they call marriage.* Thank you, Adam. Thank you, Eve.

Now, what is so hopeful about their story—Adam and Eve's, that is, which is our story, too, all of us—is that God came looking for them. They had made a real mess of things, those two, and now they were holding up a fig leaf with one hand and using the other to point an accusing finger, and God got down on his hands and knees and came looking for his children. In order to rescue them. "Adam, where are you?" (Genesis 3:9). Why, you could retrace these steps in every marriage that has ever followed: Some sort of Eden-like romance, or at least the promise of Eden in young love, and then a hard fall, followed by hiding, blaming, and reproach.

And the grace of God offering a second chance.

Hope

Fast-forward from the scene at the kitchen table—now twenty-two years ago—to October eighth, our twenty-fifth wedding anniversary. Friends and family gathered to celebrate with us. We felt a celebration was in order. One after another, people offered the most beautiful toasts—thanking us for our marriage, telling us story after story of how our love had changed their lives. Our sons also spoke, and this is what they said:

Dad, Mom, we are gathered here to celebrate your twenty-fifth wedding anniversary, not because we have to or because we should, but because your marriage is worth celebrating. It has only been as we have gotten older that the impact your marriage has had on us really became clear. Standing here now we want to thank you both for being who you are, and for loving each other in a world where most parents don't. You gave us the opportunity to grow up in a loving home, with loving parents. That is amazing. St. Augustine said, "Love is the beauty of the soul." You really are two beautiful people in love, and it is and has been such a gift to grow up knowing that is a possibility. So, not only do we congratulate you, but we thank you.

Stasi and I were speechless. And just a little embarrassed.

We had no idea that our marriage had been *noticed,* let alone had such a powerful effect on the lives of the people we love. Because the journey is taken step-by-step, we had not realized just how far we had come. I found myself wondering, *How did we get here? When did this happen?*

There is of course a story to tell, a wild and redemptive story that has at its center the Gospel of Jesus Christ. For if it is anything at all, the Gospel of Christianity is an offer of restoration. God knows that the human race is in bad shape. He knows our lives are nowhere near what we once dreamed of. He knows what it's like, living as we all do now, so far from Eden. It breaks his heart. So he comes himself to planet earth, this vale of tears, comes to do for us what none of us could accomplish on our own. He comes as Immanuel—God *with* us—and look what begins to happen. The blind receive their sight, the outcast is brought home, families are reconciled, the lame walk, and the dead are raised. These aren't just Bible stories; they are illustrations. God is demonstrating his power and his *intentions.*

He comes to heal. He comes to save.

"For the Son of Man came to seek and to save what was lost."

(LUKE 19:10)

This is how Jesus describes his mission; this is how he sees it. Notice the choice of words—he says he came to seek and save "*what* was lost." All that was lost (and O, how much has been lost). Including all of the beauty and power of a marriage. Marriage was *his* idea, after all. God created marriage, and put the desire in our hearts. However else it is you think you came together, what other forces you think were at work, the hopeful truth is that marriage is something God cares deeply about—including *your* marriage. When through the prophet Malachi the Lord God of Israel says, "I hate divorce," we hear it with a shudder. But it ought to be with a surge of hope—the passion conveyed in those three words reveals how deeply he *loves* marriage, how strong his vested interests are in its success.

Therefore, we have all the resources of God's heart toward us, and all the resources of his kingdom for the restoration of what was lost in our hearts, our lives, and our marriages. We have no idea how couples make it without God's help. That is not a book we could write. Asking for your marriage to flourish without God is like asking a tree to blossom without sunshine and water. Some sort of tree might grow, but you are not going to like the looks of it. The hope we offer is that the Christian Gospel brings with it restoration and *life*.

Most of you have heard of the famous Cross, the assurance of forgiveness (and Lord knows we'll need buckets of that as we go along). In the Cross God undergoes utter forsakenness so that we will never be forsaken. He understands sorrow, pain, rejection, misunderstanding, and abandonment. But what follows is for some reason, less well-known or at least less understood—the *Resurrection,* the triumph of the life of God. This is as central to Christianity as the Cross, perhaps even more so. Because it is that *life* he offers to us.

George MacDonald explains that "the whole history is a divine agony to give divine life to creatures. The outcome of that agony . . . will be radiant life, whereof joy unspeakable is the flower."

Letting that life into a marriage is the sunshine and water for the parched tree; it is like opening all the doors and windows of a house long boarded up. Light and fresh air pouring in. Or it is like a rain shower coming to the thirsty desert. Everything bursts into bloom— the flower of joy unspeakable. The life of God brings Resurrection—a return of real love, genuine companionship, romance, joy, long suffering, and a shared mission. This is what the Scriptures mean when they tell us that "we shall be saved through his life," the life of God come into us through Jesus Christ (Romans 5:10).

Stasi and I have become best friends. We started out that way, long ago, before we married, but we lost it somewhere along the road. More than once. God has helped us find it again. We have a shared life now. We are on the same page, living for the same things. We have found our way to something beautiful. We have found that the promise of the Gospel is true.

Let Desire Return

What would it look like for the two of you to find *your* way to something beautiful?

Don't start with, *How can that happen?* How will come in time; we can help you with how. You have to begin with *desire*. Start with what is written on your heart. What was it that you once dreamed of as a young man or woman? What was it you wanted when you first fell in love?

As a woman, I [Stasi] know what I want. I want to be seen and valued for who I am, to be truly *known* by my husband. That is why I loved the movie *Titanic*. Rose's fiancé doesn't "get" Rose. He recognizes that she is unhappy but doesn't "pretend to know why." Nor does he even ask her. Jack, on the other hand, understands Rose's heart—he sees both her *outward* beauty and her *inward* beauty and because of that, he values her, cherishes her, fights for her. He sees Rose for who she truly is, and delights in her, giving her the courage to throw away a future that seemed secure for one that is completely unknown. Being deeply known by John and still loved by him, delighted in—that is a deep desire of my heart.

I also want to live my life *with* my husband, to share in the adventure of life. I don't want to be alone in my life. I want to share the inward workings of my heart and the outward details of my life—the joys and sorrows, the small ones as well as the big ones. Life can be hard, sometimes cruel, and often dangerous. To share it with my husband helps give me both the courage and the desire to rise to the occasion. In *The Scarlet Pimpernel* the hearts and lives of

Sir Percy Blakeney and his wife, Marguerite, become one when she understands the truth of his identity and joins in the higher call of his life. As she rises to play her irreplaceable role in the story and they *share* in the adventure, his life is saved and good triumphs over evil. I want to do that for John. I want to do that *with* John.

And finally, I want to lean into John's strength. When the going gets tough and the tough get going, I want to know that John is not going anywhere; that he will be there for me to lean on when I need to. And I have needed to many, many times. Just as the Dashwood sisters in *Sense and Sensibility* learn the immeasurable gift of being able to lean into the strength of Colonel Brandon's character, I too want to rest in my husband's strength. I think these are the things every woman wants.

As a man, I [John] read what Stasi just wrote and say, *Huh. Wow. That's good to know.* Because my desires are a little different. First, I want to be believed in. There's a scene in the movie *Cinderella Man* that almost brought me to tears. It's a come-from-behind story about a boxer no one thought could return. James Braddock is about to face his most brutal opponent, a Goliath who has killed men in the ring. This is the match of his life. His wife, Mae, makes her way across New York City, down into the basement of Madison Square Garden, finds "Jimmy" in the locker room simply so she can say, "Remember who you are. . . . I'm always behind you." I love that scene.

I also want Stasi to ride with me in some great adventure. You might remember the movie *The Man from Snowy River*—there's a scene I can still recall, even though it was more than twenty years ago when I first saw it. The beautiful young Jessica has gone missing; she is in danger. Her horse threw her high in the mountains. The strong young cowboy Jim finds her and rescues her. Suddenly there they are, just the two of them, miles from nowhere out in the wild beauty of the mountains. I love that scene—wild, untamed beauty, and a shared adventure.

Finally, I want beauty. I want the love described in the Song of Songs when the woman says to her lover, "Come away, my lover, and be like a gazelle or like a young stag on the spice-laden mountains" (8:14). She thinks he is amazing; she offers her beauty to him; she invites him to be the man with her. I think men will know what I'm talking about. There's a scene from the movie *Hook* that caught me off guard. Peter Pan has returned, after many long years, to Never Land. He is a grown man now. Tinker Bell—played by Julia Roberts—is thrilled to have him back. She uses her magic to zap herself into a full-sized woman, absolutely dressed to kill. Peter asks, "Wow, Tink—what's the celebration?" "You," she says.

I think these three desires are shared by every man reading this. And you, Dear Reader—what scenes have captured your heart over the years? What songs, what stories, what moments have awakened the deep desires of your heart?

You see, somewhere along the way we all lose heart in marriage. We all do. It happens to the best of us. As Dan Fogelberg sang,

Joy at the start
Fear in the journey,
Joy in the coming home
A part of the heart gets lost in the learning,
Somewhere along the road.

(DAN FOGELBERG, *"Along the Road"*)

We might find a way to manage our disappointment and we might do our best to fight off resignation, but it works its way in. We let go of what we wanted, what we dreamed of, what we were created for. We begin to settle.

Because marriage is hard, sometimes painfully hard, your first Great Battle is not to lose heart. That begins with recovering desire— the desire for the love that is written on your heart. Let desire return. Let it remind you of all that you wanted, all that you were created for.

And then consider this—what if God could bring you your heart's desire? It's not too late. It isn't too hard. You are not too far along nor are you and your spouse too set in your ways. God is the God of all hope. He is, after all, the God of the Resurrection. Nothing is impossible for him. So give your heart's desire some room to breathe.

What if the two of you could find your way to something beautiful?

That would be worth fighting for.

TWO

Love and War

The vision is always solid and reliable; the vision is always a fact.
It is the reality that is often a fraud.

—G. K. CHESTERTON

Stasi and I hadn't made love for a while.

I'm not sure of all the reasons behind that. The hectic pace of the Christmas season, probably, and the stress of our respective worlds. No, now that I think about it, those were the "cover," the distraction providing an excuse when the real issues were all that has been stirred up writing a book on marriage together. (Can you imagine doing this with your spouse? I mean, if you open that closet door who knows what will spill out onto the floor?) Pushing into questions about desire and love and disappointment has shaken us both out of that cordial détente most married couples call marriage. So it had been a while.

Sex can be such a stark barometer for a marriage.

If things are not going well in other arenas, it doesn't take long for that to manifest in bed. She didn't seem interested the past few weeks; I felt myself pulling away. The horizon looked bleak. So I prayed. I prayed yesterday that God would come into our sexuality; I prayed that his glory would fill our marriage bed. Warming to the task, I prayed he would make us both as passionate as when we were young, when it wouldn't take more than a lingering kiss for the furnaces to start blazing. Inviting God in felt like the only thing I knew to do. Flowers and candy seemed ridiculous. So I called on Higher Powers.

We made love last night. And it was good. Really, really good. For both of us. That dark chocolate sensuality between the sheets, the deep lusciousness of two bodies entwined. The soft beauty of the feminine form calling forth the strength of the masculine. We found our way back into the Garden, if only for a moment. All those tensions that pushed us apart were simply gone. We were back in love, literally plunged into love, allowing ourselves to drink deeply the elixir of love. Sex is so mythic you can't begin to describe it. Utter oneness. Unfettered desire awoken and offered and satisfied.

When it is good it is a window into Eden.

As we lay there afterward, Stasi's head on my shoulder, it seemed that time had slipped away and taken with it all that had come between us. As waves rise, swell and thunder onto the beach, then wash it clean as they recede so gently back into the sea. Lying there I knew that *This is what is true*—true of love, true of us, true of marriage. How did I forget? Why is it so easy to lose sight of what is most deeply true? I found myself realizing again that this is the woman I love, this is what I want, and this is what is true of our marriage.

How do I find this in the daily living of our lives?

There is so much set against marriage; it clouds our perception like a sandstorm. So let us return to Eden and see if we can remember together what is written deeply on our hearts, remember the story we are made for.

Our Marriages Are Part of a Larger Story

The Bible begins with a marriage, and ends with a marriage.

We never noticed that before.

Here is the story God is telling, the story that will explain our lives, the story in which all other stories find their meaning. Open the book to chapter one, page one, and suddenly—there is a marriage.

> *God put the Man into a deep sleep. As he slept he removed one of his ribs and replaced it with flesh. God then used the rib that he had taken from the Man to make Woman and presented her to the Man.*
>
> > *The Man said,*
> > *"Finally! Bone of my bone,*
> > *flesh of my flesh!*
> > *Name her Woman,*
> > *For she was made from Man."*
>
> *Therefore a man leaves his father and mother and embraces his wife. They become one flesh.*
>
> *The two of them, the Man and his Wife, were naked, but they felt no shame.*
>
> (GENESIS 2:21–25, *The Message*)

It all begins with a couple. Not some hero standing alone against the rising tide of the world. A *marriage*. A man and a woman, given to one another at the dawn of time. The human race is about to enter into its great adventure and its great struggle. As God begins the wild, terrifying, and beautiful story, we are introduced to the hero and the heroine. And they are . . . married. Well, what do you know. That's unexpected. Marriage must play some essential role in the unfolding drama.

Now flip to the end of the story.

The epic tale reaches its climax with the end of the world as we know it. After the white horse and its rider appear, after the legendary battle of Armageddon, as the whole creation reaches its dénouement, suddenly we find—a marriage.

> *Then I saw a new heaven and a new earth . . . and I saw the Holy City, the new Jerusalem, coming down out of heaven from God, prepared as a bride beautifully dressed for her husband. . . . Come with me! I will show you the bride, the wife of the Lamb.*
>
> (REVELATION 21:1–2, 9)

There in the closing pages of the book of Revelation, as the saga comes to a breathtaking finish, trumpets sound and a feast is held—a *wedding* feast. Marriage ushered in the age of man in Genesis, and now marriage ushers in the Kingdom of God.

In some sense marriage *is* the Kingdom of God, the purpose for which God has been fighting lo these many ages—the marriage of Christ and his church, that is. All other marriages end here, for God will be united with his people.

And so we see from start to finish, the part of this great story we have been given to play begins and ends with a marriage.

Holy cow. What have we been missing here? Why does God give marriage such a central part in this story of redemption? What does he know that we don't yet see?

This Is a Love Story

Well, let's begin here—this is a love story, dear friends.

God is love, the apostle John tells us, and then he says it again so that we don't forget, "God is love, and the one who abides in love abides in God" (1 John 4:16). Love is the single most defining quality of his character and his life. God is a passionate, and jealous, lover. (Is there really any other kind?) Out of his love he creates us for love. "We love, because he first loved us" (1 John 4:19). The Scriptures tell us we are made in God's image. You'll notice that we human beings are, above all else, deeply and profoundly *relational*. Because he is. God is Trinity, a fellowship of love. Love and intimacy are the core of his being, and so he gives to each of us a heart like his. When God does this, he reveals our deepest purpose—to love and to be loved.

This is, after all, a love story.

Why else would love be the deepest yearning of our hearts?

Isn't love the greatest joy of human existence? And the loss of love our greatest sorrow? Do not the two great commands confirm this? "Love the Lord your God with all your heart . . . and your neighbor as yourself" (Luke 10:27). Love, for this is your destiny. Love God, and love each other. The banners that fly over God's kingdom are the banners of love. It's not about Bible study and faithful church attendance, not even dutiful marriage. Take the heart out of all that and it will absolutely kill you. This story is meant to be a passionate love affair. "I have loved you," God says, "with an everlasting love; I have drawn you with loving-kindness" (Jeremiah 31:3).

We live in a love story, a romance written before the foundations of the earth. Aren't the most impassioned pleas of the Bible directed toward love?

"Love one another sincerely, from the heart."

(1 PETER 1:22)

"Beloved, let us love one another."

(1 JOHN 4:7)

"A new command I give you—love one another."

(JOHN 13:34)

You begin to get the sense that love is central to this story. We are urged to love, commanded to love, warned to love, implored to love. With abandon. Over and over and over again. Good grief! Why?

Because of what is at stake.

You see, this love story takes place in the midst of a terrible war.

A War Story

Think again of all the great fairy tales. Notice that in every last one of them, the kingdom hangs in the balance; evil is advancing upon the land. What are they trying to tell us? The very thing the Bible has been trying to tell us.

The honeymoon of Adam and Eve—and their shared honeymoon with God—is barely under way when the evil one snakes in with a plan to break everyone's heart. The devil convinces the two newly-weds that they cannot trust the heart of God. He deceives them. They break the one command God gave. They reach, they fall. The beautiful kingdom is overthrown by darkness, into darkness. The circle of intimacy is broken.

> *This is why I weep*
> *and my eyes overflow with tears.*
> *No one is near to comfort me,*
> *no one to restore my spirit.*
> *My children are destitute*
> *because the enemy has prevailed.*
>
> (LAMENTATIONS 1:16)

Think Auschwitz. Think the killing fields of Cambodia. This beautiful love story is about to become an unspeakable tragedy.

But this is a people plundered and looted, all of them trapped in pits or hidden away in prisons. They have become plunder, with no one to rescue them; they have been made loot, with no one to say, "Send them back" (Isaiah 42: 22). Now "the whole world lies under the control of the evil one" (1 John 5:19).

But love is more powerful than Satan thought. God will not abandon his beloved, even though we have abandoned him. He comes for us. He fights to win us back.

> *The Lord will march out like a champion,*
> *like a warrior he will stir up his zeal;*

with a shout he will raise the battle cry
and will triumph over his enemies. . . .
Since you are precious and honored in my sight,
and because I love you,
I will give nations in exchange for you,
and peoples in exchange for your life. . . .
Bring my sons from afar
and my daughters from the ends of the earth—
everyone who is called by my name,
whom I created for my glory,
whom I formed and made.

(ISAIAH 42:13, 43:4–7)

In the world's darkest moment, love shines through. In spite of betrayal, idolatry, and chronic unbelief on our part, God loves us and pursues us. And his love wins the ransom of mankind. Jesus of Nazareth—the great Prince, son of the King—comes and gives his life to rescue his beloved.

Christianity is the greatest love story the world has ever known.

All of this is still unfolding, by the way—right now, as you read these words. The great and terrible clash between the Kingdom of God and the kingdom of darkness continues. They are fighting for the human heart. At its core this ancient struggle comes down to one question: Can a kingdom of love prevail? God insists that "love never fails" (1 Corinthians 13:8). Satan laughs. The world laughs. Something in us laughs, too. It sounds so utterly naïve. Love never fails? It seems like the most failure-prone thing on earth.

We're in This Together

God is telling a love story and the setting is war. This alone would orient you for the rest of your life if you really believed it.

But why marriage? Why does he give it such a central role?

There are many reasons we will explore; let us name two for now.

First, because we are going to need help. The vicious battle we find ourselves in is over the human heart—if you hadn't noticed—and hearts are famously vulnerable and in desperate need of sanctuary. Marriage is meant to throw the balance of power on our side. *You're going to need one another.*

> *Two are better than one,*
> *because they have a good return for their work:*
> *If one falls down,*
> *his friend can help him up.*
> *But pity the man who falls*
> *and has no one to help him up!*
> *Also, if two lie down together, they will keep warm.*
> *But how can one keep warm alone?*
> *Though one may be overpowered,*
> *two can defend themselves.*
> *A cord of three strands is not quickly broken.*

(ECCLESIASTES 4:9–12)

Back in Eden, when God created Man and Woman, he fashioned us as glorious counterparts, complements, *comrades*. The heart of a man longs for a battle to fight, an adventure to live, and a beauty to rescue. Just look at the movies men love and the games little boys play. The heart of a woman longs for someone to fight for her, to play an irreplaceable role in a great adventure, and to offer beauty. Just look at the movies women love and the games little girls play. Notice how perfectly the desires of our hearts fit together. Our souls are made for oneness in the same way our bodies fit beautifully together. God designed us to bring one another passionate joy.

Now, if you could write the perfect love story, how would it unfold? Most of us have something in mind like this: "A beautiful you and a beautiful me in a beautiful place, forever!"

I am all for sneaking back into Eden. If we could find a way to lift our marriage up into paradise, we would all give a king's ransom to do it. But then what? *Then what?*

If there were nothing else to the story but gazing in one another's eyes, we would be bored senseless. Tahiti for a week is a relief; Tahiti for a month is healing; Tahiti day after day with no end—why, we would be climbing the walls of our little hut. For it is also in the heart of a man and a woman to share some sort of quest, to fight some great battle *together*.

(And if we can't find a great battle, we seem to start one with each other, as if to satisfy the itch.)

In all of the great stories the boy and girl are thrown together in a great adventure they did not choose, and they desperately need each other if they are going to make it through. Shasta and Aravis are driven together by the lion; Mossy and Tangle are sent on a quest with the Golden Key; Hansel and Gretel, holding hands for fear, are making their way through the dark woods; Beauty and the Beast are learning to love so that they both might be free. Even Jack and Jill need each other to get that pail of water. We love those tales; they are loved all over the world.

But most of you haven't yet made the connection. The reason your heart leaps to these stories is because they are telling you about *your* story.

Really.

Your marriage is part of a larger story, too, a story as romantic as any that has ever stirred your heart, and at least as dangerous. The sooner you come to terms with this, the sooner you can understand what is happening in your marriage.

We cheer on the hero and the heroine because we can see what is at stake—the kingdom hangs upon their success. Yet we haven't anything close to this sort of clarity in our own marriages; we would be hard-pressed to name one thing that hangs in the balance, apart from our sanity and Grandmother's silver.

I'll wager that 90 percent of the confusion, misunderstanding, struggle, and disappointment in marriage is due to the fact that we do not understand what God is up to.

When I look back at the early years of our marriage, I think we both thought the story went like this: "Love God, love each other, and it'll all work out!" It was an extraordinarily naïve view of the world, though an extraordinarily popular one. Why is it that nearly every love story turns from a scenic romance into a desperate struggle? It is because that is the Story we find ourselves in. We are created to live in a great and terrifying story, and a great and terrifying story is precisely what we have.

"If two lie down together, they will keep warm." The picture is one of soldiers, who from time immemorial have lain down back-to-back at night, in order to keep warm in the field. God gave us to each other because we need someone to watch our back. We need someone to pick us up when we fall. How different would it be if we went to bed each night with the vision of two comrades lying down together in the midst of a glorious campaign? This is the reality, whether we see it or not.

Which leads us to the second reason God created marriage and gave it such a crucial place in the Great Love Story.

A Passion Play

When you look at a marriage what do you see? A man and a woman.

But there is more here than meets the eye.

According to Scripture, marriage is the mythic play of the love of God for his people:

> Follow God's example, therefore, as dearly loved children and walk in the way of love, just as Christ loved us and gave himself up for us as a fragrant offering and sacrifice to God. . . . Husbands, love your wives, just as Christ loved the church and gave himself up for her to make her holy. . . . "For this reason a man will leave his father and mother and be united to his wife, and the two will become one flesh."

This is a profound mystery—but I am talking about Christ and the church.

(EPHESIANS 5:1, 25, 31–32)

God created marriage as a living, breathing portrait laid out before the eyes of the world so that they might see the story of the ages. A love story, set in the midst of desperate times. It is a story of redemption, a story of healing; it is a story of love. God gives us marriage to illustrate his heart toward us. It is the deepest and most mythic reality in the world—that love is true, that God pursues us.

Our love is meant to be a picture of both his love and his fight. The masculine and the feminine, the courage and sacrifice, and yes, the blood, sweat, and tears—these play out for us and for the world the story of truest Love and his Beloved. God is fighting for the hearts of his people. He is a valiant king and lover, who will see his people free.

> *For Zion's sake I will not keep silent,*
> *for Jerusalem's sake I will not remain quiet,*
> *till her vindication shines out like the dawn,*
> *her salvation like a blazing torch.*
> *The nations will see your vindication,*
> *and all kings your glory;*
> *you will be called by a new name*
> *that the mouth of the Lord will bestow.*
> *You will be a crown of splendor in the Lord's hand,*
> *a royal diadem in the hand of your God.*
> *No longer will they call you Deserted,*
> *or name your land Desolate.*
> *But you will be called Hephzibah,*
> *and your land Beulah;*
> *for the Lord will take delight in you,*
> *and your land will be married.*

As a young man marries a young woman,
so will your Builder marry you;
as a bridegroom rejoices over his bride,
so will your God rejoice over you.

(ISAIAH 62:1–5)

God is a great lover, and he created marriage to play out on this earth a daily, living, breathing portrait of the intimacy he longs for with his people. Gulp. This is why it has such a central role. It is a kind of incarnation, *a passion play* about the love and union between Jesus and his beloved.

Which might help you appreciate why the fury of hell has been unleashed against it. God is telling a love story and the setting is war.

Pause for just a moment. God chooses *marriage* as the image of his love for his people, and our love for him?! I am dumbfounded. You're trusting us with *what*?

Then again, he gave the Church the mission of evangelizing the world, insisting that unless we do it the job will not get done. It is a mission of staggering consequence, and God hands the whole thing over to the Church, for heaven's sake—meaning, your aunt Gladys and her knitting club, the delicate parson and his domineering wife, the boys making a wreck just now of the Sunday school room, Henry the janitor who will not open the building for you because it is after hours and you haven't got a note from the trustees. These are the people God sends forth in his bid to save the world.

It helps you appreciate the stakes he loves to play at. If you look again at the stories God writes, they are nearly always tales of desperate battles against insurmountable odds by the most unlikely heroes in the world. And nearly always, a last-minute rescue: Noah and his little family put out upon an endless sea. David in a do-or-die charge against the brute Philistine; Daniel in the lion's den. Esther—in a bid to save her people—risks the head upon her shoulders on the

34

chance that the king is in a good mood. The Savior of the world at the breast of a teenage girl. The sheer number and consistency of these stories is unyielding and *unnerving*.

Your marriage, by the way, is being written by the same Author.

Coming Back to Our Senses

"The doctor just called."

Stasi doesn't need to say "Hi, it's me." We know each other's voice so well we could find one another in a bus station blindfolded. Besides, we have both been waiting for the call.

"What did he say?"

Her feminine plumbing has been coming undone, the result of giving birth to three very large baby boys. But there have been attending complications, troubling signs on the ultrasound, and the doctor insisted on taking a biopsy of her uterine wall. We waited a week for the results, each of us fending off the knowledge that her mother died of cancer, holding our breath knowing the pain of friends who have recently been through it.

"The biopsy was normal."

I couldn't speak. The profound and utter relief washing over me rendered me speechless.

It's funny how a simple phone call can yank you from the mundane—I was catching up on e-mail—into something so much bigger. When the prospect of cancer came up a few weeks ago, it was really disrupting. I realized I had been lured over the years—when times got rough—into thinking life would be easier without Stasi. God yanks me out of that with the sudden prospect that I *could* lose her. In a moment all the little things that were bugging me seemed trivial. My perspective was jolted to a higher level—a *truer* level.

Looking at my marriage is something I don't do much, for the same reason I have been dodging the recent postcards from my dentist ("Where have you been? You're overdue for a checkup!"). I have come to realize that my posture toward my marriage is that posture of détente, which I confessed earlier—a cordial peace accord in which we have both conceded a good deal of desire in exchange for smoother daily operations.

It dawns on me that I relate to my marriage like I relate to my health. I do the bare minimum to get by, hoping to get away with my indulgences and my neglect, throwing down some communication and a bit of romance now and then, like I take vitamins as a sort of insurance policy. I ignore my health, for the most part, and hope for the best.

We do this all the time, we humans do—we lose track of what matters. So God sends us disruptions in order to jolt us back to our senses. Sometimes the disruption comes in the form of desire—a longing for life as it was meant to be. Sometimes the disruption comes in the form of crisis. Or simply unhappiness. We realize we have drifted apart. Sometimes we catch a glimpse of what we long for in the eyes of another man or woman, and it startles us like turbulence at thirty thousand feet.

Our poverty is this lack of vision, this *incoherence,* and this above all else is why we so easily lose heart. It is absolutely crippling.

We must regain a vision for our marriage. We must recover the truth of the story we are living in and the role we have been given to play. The recovery of our marriage from the precipice of divorce (more than once) and the courage to push through all sorts of obstacles to find something beautiful—all of this has come to us as we have come to understand and embrace the nature of the story we are living in.

The Glory of Marriage

There is no place like marriage for those desires that God set in our hearts back in Eden—for battle, beauty, and a shared adventure; the desire for intimacy, companionship, and love—to come true. Friendship is a runner-up; friendship is one of life's greatest gifts. But it lacks the constancy of marriage, the daily-ness, the covenantal bond, and the consummation of sexual intimacy. It also lacks the potential to provide for the greatest transformation, our sanctification.

Now, name one thing in the entire created world more precious than a human heart.

It can't be done.

You might say "love," but that would be silly because we cannot love without a heart. You might point to some immortal work of art, or breathtaking sacrifice, or some noble feat of arms, but none of those could have happened without the human hearts behind them. Even the highest heights of worship cannot be realized without the heart. There is, of course, the surpassing greatness of the Gospel, and the Cross, but the Gospel is the story of God ransoming and restoring human hearts. Without the heart, the Gospel cannot achieve its intent. The heart is God's most magnificent creation, and the prize over which he fights the kingdom of darkness.

Now consider this—marriage is the sanctuary of the heart.

You have been entrusted with the heart of another human being. Whatever else your life's great mission will entail, loving and defending this heart next to you is part of your great quest.

Marriage is the privilege and the honor of living as close to the heart as two people can get. No one else in all the world has the opportunity to know each other more intimately than do a husband and wife. We are invited into their secret lives, their truest selves; we come to know their nuances, their particular tastes, what they think is funny, what drives them crazy. We are entrusted with their hopes and dreams, their wounds, and their fears.

An incredible honor is bestowed on the one to whom we pledge our lives and a deep privilege is given to us as well. Not only is marriage good for a person (it adds an average of seven years to the life of a man and three to a woman), but married people as a whole say their lives are happier than those who are single. Married people are healthier, and better off financially. And the impact of a lasting marriage upon their children is sobering. Children of divorce do not fare nearly so well in life as those who grew up in an intact family.

And why is this? Because we bear the image of God, we are made in the image of Love. We are created to love and be loved. And there is no greater context, no better opportunity to really love someone and to be loved by them throughout an entire lifetime than you will find in marriage. Of course it is dangerous as well—the two always go together. There is no greater place for damage, too, because there is no greater place for glory. God uses marriage to bring us the possibility of the deepest joys in life; Satan tries to use it for destruction.

Without you, your spouse will not become the man or the woman that God intends him or her to be and the Kingdom of God will not advance as it is meant to advance. Your spouse plays the most vital role in your life. You play the most critical role in your spouse's life. No one will have a greater impact on your spouse's soul than you. No one has greater access to your spouse's heart than you. *This is an enormous honor.*

Pause a moment; take a deep breath. Let that reality sink in a little deeper—you are the human being who plays the most significant role in your spouse's life. It is not your spouse's mother or father. It is not your spouse's favorite teacher, author, or pastor. It is you. It is a sobering truth, isn't it. You are on holy ground. You matter more than you thought.

The Cost of Marriage

Being married costs you everything. Tears. Nights of sleep. Incredible vulnerability and sacrifice. It causes you to take a deeper look inside your heart and soul, your desires and your personality. It hurts. It is not easy. But that does not come as a surprise to you. You already know that!

Of course loving costs everything—look at the Cross. But loving is *always* worth it.

We all know that loving is hard. Marriage is hard. It is hard because it is *opposed.* The devil hates marriage; he hates the beautiful picture of Jesus and his Bride that it represents. He hates love and life and beauty in all its forms. The world hates marriage. It hates unity and faithfulness and monogamy. Our flesh is not our ally here either—it rebels when we put others before ourselves. Our flesh hates dying.

But God loves marriage! The Holy Trinity is for it. God loves intimacy, friendship, unity, self-sacrifice, laughter, pleasure, joy, and the picture of the Sacred Romance that you have the opportunity to present to the watching world. God is with you. He is for you. He commands you to love and he says that with him and in him all things are possible. Not easy. But possible.

Marriage is going to ask everything of you, and that is why you must have a vision for it. (Why do you suppose God has us seal the bond with vows, for heaven's sake?)

So there you have it—we live in a great love story, set in the midst of war. We need each other—desperately. We have been entrusted with the heart of another human being. Our loving will prove to the world that love is real. We will play out before watching eyes the Great Love Story of the ages.

THREE

A Perfect Storm

I fell into a burning ring of fire.

—— JOHNNY CASH

So . . . God creates Adam and Eve, Man and Woman. He brings them close together, about as close as two living beings can get. Murderously close. He puts them in a marriage. And they all live happily ever after. Right?

Why are you laughing? What was that cynical snort?

Just this morning Stasi and I were talking about marriages we know, and we came to a sobering realization: We can't name one single marriage that hasn't been through deep waters in the last three years. Not one. And we know a lot of people, and therefore a lot of marriages. Between family, friends, church, work, and the neighborhood, you would think we would be able to point to some couple who is trouble free. We can't find one. *Not one.* Every single married couple we know is either currently struggling, or has just passed through some major struggle, or has thrown in the towel.

Now, we would love to blame all the hardships of marriage on the Great Battle swirling around us, but that would not be altogether honest—would it? There are other dynamics at work. The sooner we understand them, the sooner we will be able to see why "love" can so quickly turn to "war" between husband and wife. We do have an enemy who is hell-bent on destroying us. But we *also* have ourself

40

and our spouse to contend with—each of us with a history, a personality, and a unique approach to making life work.

It can feel like desperately trying to mix oil and water. Or something more combustible.

Opposites Do Attract

Stasi likes to talk. Especially in the morning, as we're heading into the day. Or in the evening, when we are getting ready for bed. I'll be standing in the kitchen in the morning, and she'll start a conversation from the bedroom and she'll just carry right on even though I am running the blender and no rabbit could possibly hear a thing she's saying. Then she'll walk into the room and ask, "Well?" Or at night, she'll wait until I'm brushing my teeth to start telling me a story (from a room away) and I've got the sound of a car wash in my head and I can't discern half of what she's holding forth on.

It drives me nuts.

Like many married couples, Stasi has "her" car and I have "my" car (a Honda and a Ford pickup, respectively). We'll be headed off on some errand or other, jump into my car, and the first thing she'll do is start changing the channel on the radio, or start punching the buttons to change the temperature. I'll give her a "look" like *What are you doing?* And she'll say, "What?" She doesn't even get it.

It drives me nuts.

And then there are the lights. Whatever room we are in, Stasi likes the lights dim. (I call her a salamander—she likes it dark and cool.) I, on the other hand, love a room as bright as can be. Now, we'll be sitting in the room together and Stasi will just get up and dim down the lights.

Drives me absolutely nuts. . . .

John likes to smell things before he eats them. Like a cat. He'll open a box of cereal and smell it before he takes a bite. I'll offer to share my bag of chips with him and he'll smell them before taking one. He does it with fruit, with milk, a jar of mustard, with anything that could possibly in its lifetime go bad.

It drives me crazy. And he has this habit of getting up and walking out of the room without saying where he's going or why. We will be in the middle of family time together, and he'll just get up and walk out. I'll go look for him and find him in the garage doing something. "What?" he says. He'll even leave the house in the same fashion, just up and go out the door and be gone without a good-bye or "I'm running to the office" or anything.

We were on a rare date, on our way to see a movie, and we were running a bit late. It had taken me a little longer to gather myself together before leaving—John calls this "futzing"—but really, I reasoned, we should have plenty of time. If we hurry. We pulled into the parking lot on this crowded Friday night and approached an open parking space. *Great, this will be quick,* I think! John passed it by. He continued down the row passing by two more perfectly acceptable parking spaces and tried another row. He was driving around searching for the *best* spot he could find.

And he was driving me crazy.

I am a woman who needs and craves *structure.* I function best within parameters; a schedule, albeit a flexible one, is my friend. In managing our home, I keep a large master calendar. When are the bills due? Who has what going on when and what does that require of whom? Particularly *me.* I don't like to have things sprung on me at the last moment. Don't throw me a surprise party. It will not go well. When my days are topsy-turvy, I feel unbalanced inside. I am happiest when I know what's coming and when, when decisions have been made, and when I can check things off my "to do" list! I don't handle change well at all. John is the exact opposite—he *likes* choices, open-ended discussions. When he talks, it is not because he has made up his mind—like me—but because he is thinking through his options. He likes to go with the flow.

It drives me crazy.

Now, add to our personality differences the fact that he's a *man* and I'm a *woman*. You get two people so opposite from one another they are often a complete mystery to the other.

I like to relax in a hot bath, with lavender bubbles. This doesn't appeal to John at all, not one bit. Sometimes when he's stressed I'll suggest a hot bath and he'll look at me like I suggested he paint his fingernails. I enjoy watching cake decorating shows. John is hooked on *Man Vs. Wild*. He likes the occasional cigar. I don't like the smell. I love scented candles. John abhors them. A treat for me is getting a pedicure; an amazing day for John is going bow hunting.

And we live together. In the same house. It's a wonder we don't kill each other. Sometimes we drive each other crazy simply by being ourselves. Puddleglum had it right:

> *But we all need to be very careful about our tempers, seeing all the hard times we shall have to go through together. Won't do to quarrel, you know. At any rate, don't begin it too soon. I know these expeditions usually* end *that way: knifing one another.*
>
> (C. S. LEWIS, *The Silver Chair*)

It's a wonder we haven't come to knives.

Learning to live with our opposite and all their little quirkinesses is part of learning to love. "Love it is a rock," Shawn Mullins sings, "smoothed over by a stream." We want love to be stable and immovable, like a rock. Steady and sure. But that stream part is another matter. Some force constantly washing over us, smoothing our rough edges. We don't much go in for that. But let's face it—we've all got some roughness to our personalities, don't we? We've all got a good bit of smoothing over to do. For this wonderful process, God gives us . . . each other. Marriage is the rushing stream God uses to shape us into more loving people.

The Second Great Shock

For some reason, I [John] remember this conversation vividly. We were driving up Interstate 25 through Colorado Springs, a young friend and I, when he made the following pronouncement: "I'm so glad that Megan's not broken." He was talking about the girl he was about to get engaged to. I tried to suppress the raising of my eyebrows, said nothing, in hopes he would continue with his train of thought. "I mean, think of all the gals in our community—most of them are really a mess. Megan is not. She's good." I just kept looking forward, nodded, said something like, "That's great." He wasn't ready for what I had to say. I mean, enjoy the balloon while you can; I don't need to be the one to pop it. Inside, something sad sort of sighed. *Brother, you are in for one heck of a shock.*

It is six years later, and he would describe this past year as the most difficult of his entire life. Turns out there was a lot more brokenness to Megan than he thought.

There always is.

The first big shock we receive in marriage is that it is hard. The second great shock usually follows hard on the heels of the first—that we are, both of us, a royal mess. Why is he so defensive? Why doesn't she enjoy sex? How come he withers under criticism? Why is she so clingy? What is this simmering rage just under the surface? Where did this addiction come from? Why won't you talk to me? Who *are* you?!

Probably the truest place to pick up the story of any marriage is many years beforehand, in the story of the little boy and the little girl who will one day fall in love and pledge their lives to each other. I [Stasi] brought into our marriage a wounded heart and deep, profound insecurity. The defining wound in my life came when I was three years old while sitting at the kitchen table watching my mother prepare dinner. She told me for the first time, but not the last, how devastated she had been when she learned she was pregnant with me, how she wept to learn that I was coming. Her words pierced my heart with the message: "*You are a disappointment, your very existence causes pain.*"

Like every other little girl, I came into the world with a question deep in my heart that went something like, "*Do you delight in me?*" The answer I received from my mom's pain was "No." As profound of an impact a mother has on her daughter, her father has an even greater one. So, as a child, like every other child, I primarily brought my heart's question to my dad.

As a traveling salesman, my father would be gone for two weeks at a time, then be home for a weekend, then hit the road again for two weeks, then be home for another weekend. He was not unkind to me when he was around—he just wasn't around. A blossoming alcoholic with a difficult marriage, my father would stop for a few drinks at a bar or even a neighbor's before entering our front door. This was his routine until I was ten years old. After that, his promotion and his souring relationship with my mom kept him at the office for long hours. I would go many days without seeing him, thinking he was out of town; he was simply staying away.

The message I received as a little girl in our flailing family was: "Don't rock the boat or this boat will go down." I didn't feel delighted in; I didn't even feel seen. The last of four children born too close together to an overwhelmed mother and an absent father, I learned early to keep to myself; hiding my true self from the eyes of my busy parents. I believed if I needed too much or caused discomfort to my parents, the wobbly world as I knew it would topple. I didn't want to be the one to cause our family to sink. The world is a dangerous and precarious place; too many wrong moves on my part and I would destroy it. I brought all that into our marriage.

I believed John loved me, kind of, but I was perched in wariness just waiting for the other shoe to drop. I believed to my core that I was a disappointment, so I desperately tried to be the woman that I thought John wanted me to be. I would not offer my husband my true self because I believed that the truest me would not be wanted. I tried to figure out how to never rock the boat in my relationship with John, who was at the time of our union an unrepentant perfectionist—and it couldn't be done. He corrected me on how I chopped vegetables for soup. He re-ironed shirts that I ironed for him. His smallest dissatisfaction with anything pertaining to me was interpreted by my wounded heart to mean *"I am utterly disappointed in you."*

I loved my husband but I was afraid. And so I hid. By gaining weight. By refusing to share my true feelings. By refusing to confront John on things he needed to be confronted on. I developed a way of relating in my marriage that protected me from further wounding. It seemed like the perfectly reasonable thing to do. And it almost destroyed my marriage.

The defining wound of my life [John here] was my father's alcoholism. Every little boy carries an essential question in his heart, too, but it is unique to men: "Do I have what it takes?" And a little boy looks to his daddy for the answer to that question.

My father wound (and multiple wounds thereafter) is abandonment—no one will ever be there for you. It's one of the ruling sentences of my life. That's my brokenness; there's a long history of that and a lot of story to it, but enough story that my young heart came to believe that to be pretty true. That's my reality, that's the way the world works—no one will ever really be there for you. You are on your own.

I discovered pretty early on that I was smart enough and articulate enough to make life work just fine on my own. I became a frightened, driven perfectionist, certain that love does not last and committed to self-protection under the banner: "I will never need anyone."

A woman with deep wounds of disappointment marries a man she cannot possibly please; her fear that she will never really be loved meets his commitment to never need anyone. That's like someone with a fear of heights taking a job cleaning windows on the Empire State Building. A man with deep abandonment wounds from his father's addiction marries a woman whose deep addiction will cause her to withdraw from him. His fear that what he has to offer will never be enough meets the chasm in her heart that no amount of love can fill. The way these things play into each other is chilling. You could not script a more frightening scenario.

Opposites attract all right—our mutual brokenness is drawn together like a match and gunpowder.

And God is in that, by the way. He is the author of your marriage. He planned this.

Our brokenness combines with our sin and produces a style of relating. An approach to life, which to us feels so utterly justified and so perfectly reasonable, but in fact is the very thing that will destroy us and all those around us.

What Is God Thinking?!

When it comes to high-level expeditions, one piece of advice that veterans unanimously urge is this: "Choose your tent mate carefully." For you are going to spend weeks to months on end shut in by foul weather in the forced intimacy of a tiny fabric cocoon with this person. By the time it is over, everything about him will drive you mad—the way he eats, the way he breathes, the way he hums show tunes, or the way he picks his nails. To keep yourselves from a Donner party ending, you must start with people you are utterly compatible with.

God does the opposite—he puts us *with* our opposite. Our mutual brokenness plays off each other so perfectly that it is frightening. It's like throwing a dog and a cat in a dryer. Is he absolutely mad? Why would God do such a thing?

Because marriage is a divine conspiracy.

It is a conspiracy divinely arranged and with divine intent.

God lures us into marriage through love and sex and loneliness, or simply the fact that someone finally paid attention—all those reasons that you got married in the first place. It doesn't really matter, he'll do whatever it takes. He lures us into marriage and then he uses it to *transform us*.

Come back to the fairy tales—in every one of those stories, the boy and the girl each carry a fatal flaw. If they refuse their transformation—which is essential to the plot of the story—they'll never make it. Evil will win, they will lose heart and split up, and there will be no happily ever after. Shasta—given to feeling sorry for himself—is defensive. Aravis—holding a rather high view of herself—is dismissive. They are continually at odds, and the *Chronicles of Narnia* story cannot reach its climax until Shasta stops grousing and Aravis humbles herself. In *Beauty and the Beast,* Beauty is a prima donna and the Beast has anger management issues. She must find her courage and he must find his tenderness. In every one of those stories, happily ever after waits upon a particular turn of events, at the center of which is the character's transformation.

This all goes back to Adam and Eve. They fell, of course, and their sin is *our* sin; it has infected men and women ever since.

As a man, Adam was endowed with the image of God primarily in his strength—a strength given him for the benefit of others. It's not about big muscles, but about *inner* strength. Notice that when men fail, they tend to fail in one of two ways—either they become passive and silent, or they become domineering and violent. They either don't offer their strength or they wield it in harmful ways. I [John] did both—I was utterly passive when it came to offering Stasi intimacy; I ran and hid at work. And I was practically violent in my driven perfectionism.

As a woman, God endowed Eve with beauty—an *inner* beauty often expressed as tenderness and vulnerability. Notice that when women fail they tend to either become controlling or desperately needy. Either they refuse to offer vulnerability or they ask their man to fill the ache in their soul. I [Stasi] did both—my weight was a way of controlling my world and insulating myself from intimacy. My fear that I was a disappointment kept me from offering my true self. And yet I would look to John to fill me.

We all have a way that we *do* life. We might call it our personality, or our natural bent—the way we handle pressure, the way we listen, the way we look for happiness, the way we control our world. We didn't sit down one day and willfully choose to adopt it but it remains a choice nonetheless. Call it our style of relating. It is a carefully crafted approach to life—especially to relationships— that colors the way we work, the way we love, the way we respond, and the way we simply have a conversation with people. This can be quite an epiphany—you have a style of relating designed to make life work for you!

Our style of relating is born out of brokenness and sin, and it is *the Number One Thing* that gets in the way of real love and real companionship, the shared adventure and all the beauty of marriage. It is really this simple. The number one thing that gets in the way *is* your way. I don't mean insisting on getting your way—dimming the lights or finding a better parking spot. I mean your way of going about life, your style of relating.

We are, all of us, utterly committed and deeply devoted to our "style," our "way," our "approach to life." We have absolutely no intention of giving it up. Not even for love. So God creates an environment where we have to. It's called *marriage.*

Take the fundamental differences of a man and a woman. Add to this the fact that opposites attract and our peculiarities are nearly always at odds. Toss in our profound brokenness, our sin, and our style of relating. It's the perfect storm.

Now listen carefully: God wants us to be happy. He really does. "I've come," Jesus said, "that you may have life and have it to the full" (John 10:10). He simply knows that until we deal with our brokenness, our sin, and our style of relating, we aren't going to be happy. Nobody around us is going to be very happy, either. Most of what you've been experiencing in the last twelve months is God's attempt to get you to face your style of relating and repent of it.

When I was a child, I talked like a child, I thought like a child, I reasoned like a child. When I became a man, I put childish ways behind me.

(1 CORINTHIANS 13:11)

This is the old Christian understanding of the world, the understanding that happiness is the fruit of other things, chief among them our own holiness, and so we *must* undergo a transformation. We must be smoothed over. Just like the fairy tales, we must share in God's holiness before the story is finished.

This flies in the face of the more popular view of the world that's crept in recently—"the happiness view." This is the idea that frames most people's expectations of marriage (and everything else)—the view that we are here for our happiness and therefore others had better make us happy.

So it comes as quite a disruption when we begin to realize that God might have other things in mind.

Learning to Love

Life ought to be better with you than without you.

It certainly isn't supposed to be *harder,* for heaven's sake.

We described the first shock of marriage as that moment we discover it is hard, and the second shock as that moment we realize that both of us are a royal mess. This is all actually quite hopeful, because these discoveries lead us to the secret of life—we are here to learn how to love. "A new command I give to you." Jesus said, "Love one another as I have loved you" (John 15:12). This is a love story, after all. And what does learning to love look like? Well, for one thing, it looks like compassion for your spouse's brokenness while choosing to turn from your own self-protective style of relating.

We must come to face our style, of course. As men, we look to where we are passive, and where we are domineering, harsh, or violent. As women, we face where we are controlling, and where we are desperately clingy. And as God reveals these things, we make those thousand little choices to turn from our style of relating. We make deliberate choices to love. If you have been avoiding conflict, either as a passive man or a controlling woman, then you say: "Conflict is okay. Let's talk about these things. I'll go there with you." If you have been avoiding intimacy, then you say: "I need you. I don't want to be this island, this impenetrable fortress. I choose to engage." If you have been controlling, then let go of control. If you've been hiding, then come out of hiding. If you have been filled with anger, then set aside your anger and choose to be vulnerable.

Can you honestly talk together about your styles of relating? Do you even have a clue what yours is? Ask God. It can feel daunting, risky, and too vulnerable to talk with your mate about this right away. But it's a good conversation to have. Not one of judgment and accusation, but one of truth being spoken in love—to help you understand and love each other *better*.

Now, it would be very, very helpful for you both to know the story of each other's lives. Ladies, do you know the story of your husband's life? Gents, do you know the story of your wife's life?

Over the past several years, safe in the trusted confidantes of our small group, six of us took turns "sharing our story." We took an evening each, and told the story of our lives. Starting with our childhood, we spoke of memorable moments—the painful ones as well as the happy ones. We unfolded the pages of our lives. And even though each couple had been married for more than two decades, husbands and wives heard new stories that profoundly impacted them. Countless "ah ha" moments. Many tears. Much mercy.

It was a beautiful beginning to come to know one another in a deeper, more substantive way. Pieces of the puzzle of each other's personalities began to fit into place. "Oh, that's why you hate to talk on the phone" or "So, is that why you feel so defensive to me?" Now I get it. Understanding your spouse by understanding the unfolding story of their life is priceless. You can come alongside your spouse and help them to overcome difficulties so much easier and more tenderly when you understand "where they are coming from." I think when we begin to understand each other's brokenness we'll find a great deal more compassion for actions that were previously simply driving us nuts.

Making the time to really hear your husband's story or your wife's story will be time well spent. We want to encourage you to do this. Give each other a few hours. Ask questions. Listen. Invite God to guide and fill the time. It will bear so much good fruit.

From Changing You to Changing Me

We were driving home from a matinee one wintry afternoon earlier this year when John asked me, "Why do you think you are so angry?" Huh? What? Where did this come from? We were having a pleasant afternoon together when all of a sudden he asks me that! I was feeling happy—until *then*. "We're having a nice time together!" I said, rather defensively. "Why are you asking me that *now*?"

John responded, "After all our years of marriage, Stasi, I've learned that there isn't ever a good time to ask you a question like that."

Okay. True enough.

Though the timing was startling, the question wasn't. I had been talking with God just that morning about what I had become aware of inside of me—an unsettled anger, a rage really. I would feel it erupt unbidden, not in response to a situation or to a person but seemingly having a source all its own. And my anger was increasing. I was abrupt, short, abrasive with our children and with my friends. I had been damaging the relationships I cared most about for longer than I realized, and I didn't know why. I wanted to change but I wasn't able to do it on my own. I needed help. John thought it would be helpful for me to receive some counseling.

John and I talk, of course, but we have found that it's best for a husband and wife *not* to take on the role of counselor. (We have both been to counseling in the past—once during the early years of our marriage, and then both of us separately around fourteen years ago.) God provided a gifted and Spirit-filled woman who was willing and able to be strong and truthful to me, all the while staying connected in love. Reentering the counseling office this year was a great gift. God timed it in such a way that I started in the early spring, in what became a year of unprecedented loss, grief, growth, repentance, healing, and change.

God *is* changing me and I praise him for it. I can actually say the rage is mostly gone and, with it, my destructive style of relating. I am growing in knowing my true identity in Christ and my value in him like never before. I regret the pain I caused others but I am resting in the full work of Christ which is *more than enough* for me and all my failures. Becoming more fully his is freeing me to love my husband and to love the others *he* gives me, so much more in the way God desires. Healing is possible. It's available. Oh hooray.

As I tried to think of stories that illustrated the wounding I received from my father, I couldn't think of any that had weight to them. Stories that have brought me to tears in prior years now seem small and really insignificant. Jesus has healed my broken heart, and he has removed the sting of death from my growing-up years. I remember the situation, the words, but the memories hold no grief.

But God is going even further.

When I think of my father now, I think of how much he loved me. I am remembering small moments, little presents, kind words, and tiny acts which I had forgotten. I am remembering his laughter and his many invitations to me to engage with him. Conversations. Ping-Pong games. Beach days. Practical jokes he played on my mom. I am remembering bringing him joy and being delighted in. God is rewriting my personal history! There is a lightness to my step. My heart is glad.

I didn't even know this kind of healing and freedom was available. But it is. In Heaven, my father is happy and so is my mom. There is no bitterness and no regret, only love. I am asking God to bring his healing to every area of my life and every broken place of my heart. Like the leper in Matthew, I am asking him to heal, if he is willing. And do you remember his never-changing answer to the leper, to me, to you? He says, *"I am willing"* (Matthew 8:3).

And can I [John here] say what a gift Stasi's decision to pursue her own healing has been to me and to our boys. It was a courageous and humble act, and the fruit has been wonderful. I hope she can say the same of me, though God's invitation came a little more violently in my case. Two years ago I was thrown from a horse. My left wrist was broken, my right wrist was dislocated, and I needed surgery. I was in double casts for nine weeks. I could not tie my shoes. I could not button a button. I could not cut a steak. I couldn't do a single thing for myself. It was profoundly disrupting to a man who long ago honed a style of relating where "I will never need anyone."

But what absolutely broke my heart was to see Stasi's joy in finally being needed. She lit up. She was so happy to help me tie my shoes. I felt like a burden, an imposition. But she was so happy to help me get dressed in the morning. She washed my hair. She was so happy to do things for me. And I saw in that the story of our marriage. Her joy was because it had been so rare for me to need her.

God brings in disruption to say, "John, your style of relating is horrible. It does untold damage. You have to look at this. You have to begin to let me dismantle that old style of relating and create something new in you."

My journey has involved forgiving the people who hurt me long ago, beginning with my father. It has involved renouncing the vow that I will never need anyone. And then there are the thousand little choices we make every day in which we either fall back into our old style, or we choose to live differently in order to love. I need to let Stasi help me. When I see the perfectionism springing up, I let it go. (Writing this book together has been an incredible opportunity for that.)

Two Kinds of People

Why do you look at the speck of sawdust in your brother's eye and pay no attention to the plank in your own eye? How can you say to your brother, "Let me take the speck out of your eye," when all the time there is a plank in your own eye? You hypocrite, first take the plank out of your own eye, and then you will see clearly to remove the speck from your brother's eye.

(MATTHEW 7:3–5)

There are two kinds of people in this world—the clueless and the repentant. Those who are open to looking at their life and those who are not. Folks who know they need God to change them and folks who expect everyone else to change. We have great hope for the first group. The second bunch are *choosing* ignorance; the damage they are doing is almost unforgivable.

This is why the "apply some principles" approach to marriage improvement doesn't work. So long as we choose to turn a blind eye to how we are fallen as men or women, and to the unique style of relating we have forged out of our sin and brokenness, we will continue to do damage to our marriages. We will add to our spouse's hopelessness that things will never change. You don't want to add cynicism and resignation to your marriage. You want your spouse to experience: *She is really changing! He is really thinking about his impact on me!* That inspires so much hope. It awakens so much desire. Something begins to stir in our hearts. *Wow, this could get good. I mean, we could really go places here!*

This begins to happen when we shift the focus of our energy from needing the other person to change (as in, "if only you would change, my life would be so much better!") to asking God, "How do *I* need to change?"

What would happen in your relationship if you could both make the shift from "changing you" to "changing me"?

Amazing things begin to happen as we accept the plot of the story—when we not only realize but come to *embrace* the truth that this is about our transformation. All the happiness we long for waits upon our willingness to be made holy. To learn to love.

Stasi and I are at that time in life where we are now attending the weddings of our friends' children. A new generation is taking their vows. We sit there and smile; we are genuinely happy for them. Happy they have found each other. Happy they are starting out on their journey.

We also know that these newly married couples have no idea what they are getting themselves into. That is part of the smile. Now, we're not sadists. The years have simply reconciled us to the fact that we are all here for our transformation.

And we understand that there is no place on earth quite like marriage for the kind of transformation God is after.

FOUR

The Greatest Gift You Can Give

The only person that can satisfy the aching abyss of the human heart is Jesus Christ.

—OSWALD CHAMBERS

I hate Valentine's Day. There, I said it.

Most of the guys reading this just thought, *Yes! I can't believe he said that.*

Most of the women just thought, *What a jerk! I can't believe he said that.*

But it's true. I hate Valentine's Day. And Stasi loves it; it's one of her favorite holidays. (God, what are you thinking?!) I hate being told, "Today, you will be romantic. Today, you will be amazing. Today, you will 'Get It All Right.' And tonight, you will arrange for one of the most romantic evenings you two will have this year. Tonight, sex will be on a level with the Hallelujah chorus. Hollywood will have wished they had filmed this day."

Who wants to live under that kind of pressure?

It's like going to bed promising yourself, "Tomorrow, when I wake up, I will be happy. I will be kind. I will be generous. I will

57

be an amazing person. Tomorrow is going to be the best day of my life." It might. You might.

But I doubt it.

The rule of human nature seems to be this: The harder you push, the more the heart flees. It is Newton's "Third Law of the Soul": For every action there is an equal and opposite reaction. (This could save a lot of marriages, by the way, so pay attention.) The more we demand the heart to show up, the more it disappears. We may try hard to Get It All Right, out of fear or guilt (like most guys on Valentine's Day), or maybe even out of a desire to be good. But that is not the same as loving. "I'm taking you to dinner because I'm supposed to. I'll kiss you good night because I'm supposed to." What woman wants that?

Now to be fair, a good bit of this pressure is cultural, the whole "We can make a million by making the guy feel guilty" thing. It is marketing brilliance. I mean, it works. Guys want to come through. We are made to come through. We feel our best when we are coming through. And we feel like a jerk when we are not. Now I know, I know, the women are saying, "But you don't have to do all that. I just want to know you remembered me." Right. So you're good with beers and the basketball game, right?

So I find myself dreading the approach of Valentine's Day. *Can I pull it off? Will she be happy?* And now we've got a culture crazed with the upgrade of everything. Dinner and a card used to be a home run. That sounds so blasé these days, like you barely even gave it a thought. How boring. Now you have got to make it an all-day occasion—flowers in the morning, call and sing to her at work, write a poem in the card, dinner yes (and not the same place you went to last year), but then something romantic afterward like a hot air balloon or a drive in a rented convertible up Sunset Ridge. We have blown this day way out of proportion. It has taken all the fun out of it.

And the truth is, women feel the pressure, too—the pressure to be beautiful, the pressure to have just the right earrings to go with just the right dress, the pressure to have the perfect hair—to achieve "sexy" without tipping over into "skanky." (Edith Head said your dress ought to be tight enough to show you're a woman and loose enough to show you're a lady.) A woman feels the pressure to make all the right conversation, not to order too much at dinner ("I'll just have a side salad"), and certainly don't eat it all. And a woman feels the sexual pressure coming—either to offer sex "because it's Valentine's Day" or because she wants to win her man. (Have you noticed all of the November babies? Count back nine months. I know one family in which all of their kids are November birthdays. It was one of the few "sex days" of the year.)

Real romance doesn't work like that.

Romance seems to happen not because you have turned your google-eyed attention to romance, but because the two of you are focused on other things—a beautiful fall day leads to a spontaneous walk in the woods. An evening out "just because," becomes lovely after the two of you stumble on a great little restaurant. Or maybe the two of you simply rent a movie and watch it in your sweats, but it stirs both your hearts deeply and afterward you have an amazing conversation and the intimacy makes you want to rip each other's clothes off.

Romance requires free hearts.

Pressure, on the other hand, kills everything it touches.

An Anniversary Epiphany

Our twenty-fifth wedding anniversary is coming up.

I [Stasi] have been aware for some time now that this anniversary is a big deal to me. I mean, come on—twenty-five *years*. That is a long time! We almost didn't make it past three. We had a pretty substantial crisis around ten. Twenty-five years and the fact that we actually love each other is a triumph. Hallmark makes special cards for that. Everyone knows it is your *silver* anniversary. Presents may be called for. People go on trips. My friend keeps asking me what I am getting John, and her question irritates me. I got him some fabulous cards! What more am I supposed to do? But if he wants to get me a special anniversary ring, that would be just fine by me. Huh.

Anyhow, I have been "prompting" (it should fairly be called "threatening") my children about this anniversary for the past ten years. Annually. My message has gone something like, "We are celebrating our anniversary tonight. You don't have to do anything except to say 'Happy Anniversary!' But when it's our *twenty-fifth wedding* anniversary—then you have do to do something. A party. A present. *Something!*"

Now the "Big One" is finally here, and the pressure is on. I mean ON. As the date has approached, my anxiety has increased. What if the boys do nothing? What if John does nothing? This anniversary requires more than a card (at least, for me apparently) and yes, flowers, but more please. My spirit was clamoring inside. Desire became demand. Invitation became requirement.

What I have been dreaming of is a beautiful dinner party with dancing at a gorgeous hotel. I wanted to dance with John to Josh Groban singing "When You Say You Love Me" in front of all our family and friends. (This particular desire I told John about four years ago while playing a board game, nowhere near our anniversary. I told you the pressure was on.)

I wanted flowers. I wanted to toast out of silver-engraved goblets that our children gave us. I wanted to renew our vows. I wanted to wear a show-stopping dress and look good in it. I wanted beauty. I wanted transcendence. I wanted a "golden moment."

What I didn't know was what I really wanted was my parents back.

Growing up, I wasn't a little girl who dreamt of her wedding day. I didn't plan my dress, or how many bridesmaids I would have, or what they would wear. I didn't have any idea of how many children I wanted or what I would name them. I never daydreamed about the kind of house I wanted to live in or who I wanted to live in it with. But I *did* bring one very specific desire into my marriage—what our twenty-fifth wedding anniversary would look like.

My parents' marriage didn't have a lot of golden moments in it. Not that I witnessed. I can name three. One was while we were on vacation in Banff, Canada. It was during a hike, and my parents were holding hands and then mugging for the camera; happy *together*. Another was a night when I heard giddy laughter coming from behind their closed bedroom door after we had all watched a funny movie together. And the third was when I was seventeen years old and they celebrated their twenty-fifth wedding anniversary.

My older sisters pulled off a surprise party for my parents. We spent the entire day at our neighbor's house preparing hors d'oeuvres. Then at just the right time, my sister Kelly came home and took my parents out for a celebratory drink.

When they returned it was to a house full of flowers and food, and friends and neighbors crying out their congratulations. We gave my parents engraved silver goblets that they drank champagne from. The parish priest was there and at just the right time, he led my parents in renewing their vows.

I can still picture them so clearly. I know what they were wearing, and what I was wearing. My mother was lovely and my father handsome. They were both so very genuinely *happy*. It's a moment in time held dear in my memory and my heart.

And I wanted *that*.

For our twenty-fifth wedding anniversary, I wanted that. But as the day approached, it became increasingly clear that the replica I longed for wasn't going to happen. So, in my true controlling fashion, I began to plan it. I made lists. But I wasn't glad to. I didn't want to be in charge of it. It didn't settle with me. Weren't my children supposed to throw us a surprise party? What about all my years of counsel? But now our oldest was away at college and I didn't trust them to do it. I didn't know what it was I really wanted but I wanted John to know, to understand. I wanted my sons to know. How do you ask for something, long for something, and hope for something when you don't know what the something is?

I went out and ordered a cake.

How much pressure can a woman put on her husband and her children to tend to a young place in her heart that she is unaware of? A lot of pressure, that's how much. Tons of it. Boatloads of it. I was sending John the message that he had better come through for me on this one day unlike any other. I needed him to; no, I *demanded* that he do something amazing, beautiful, and holy that I would remember and cherish for the rest of my life. And by the way, I wanted our children to hold the memory dear in their hearts and minds as well.

Oh my. What a mess.

Permit me [John here] to interject. So, I come out one morning about two weeks before the date, and Stasi is standing in the kitchen crying. *Uh oh, what's this?* I ventured into that land every man fears to go: "Honey, what's wrong?" Through tears she says, "I feel like you've ignored all of my desires for our twenty-fifth." My internal alarms start going off. I've got a crying woman on my hands and a boatload of expectations and we're maybe two weeks out and yep—I haven't given much thought to the whole party thing. I thought the boys were on that and, *Aooogha! Dive, Dive, Dive.* Every man knows this alarm. *I'm in deep kimchee, and I'd better scramble to get out of this.* So I do start scrambling. I call Sam at school and tell him I'm flying him home for the event that has yet to be planned. I send e-mails to friends to save the date. I start trying to make something happen.

Now for the happy truth of our marriage. It is never just the two of us. God is here. And just in the nick of time, he intervened.

It started with a simple conversation between John and me. (This was a few days after the tears in the kitchen.) I was upset and he could tell. John set aside his plans for his Sunday afternoon and sat down with me, pursuing my heart with gentle questions. "Sweetheart, I don't understand why you are so upset." I talked about my parents' wedding anniversary, and the tears began to flow.

What surfaced was this deep, profound longing not just for a golden moment—but for *that* Golden Moment. I began to realize that what I was longing for was to recover something from my past, something long lost. I wanted my parents young again and happy and glad to be together. I wanted to see my mother's face full of light and hope and love. I wanted my father beaming with pride. I wanted my world to line up just right where everything felt well and safe. I wanted some place in my heart that was still seventeen years old to know that everything was going to be okay and to finally stop hurting.

Up until this moment, I had no idea what was fueling all of my hopes and expectations. All I knew was that I was feeling increasingly sad, anguished, desperate, even angry about our upcoming anniversary. We prayed. Jesus came. I cried. Again. And I was able to let it all go. After about an hour I looked up and said, "I'm good. I'm okay now. I don't need a party."

Living Under So Much Pressure

I [John] was thrilled, of course, at the breakthrough. She looked up and said, "I'm fine. I don't need the Sacred Party and the Golden Memory anymore," and I'm thinking, *You're kidding me. That's what this has all been about? Hallelujah!*

I don't think most of us have any idea how much pressure we bring to our marriages.

There is the pressure one of you feels from the other to "be happy." Usually because somebody's childhood wasn't all that happy, and they can't bear even the threat of unhappiness in their marriage. Or maybe we lay on this pressure because we deeply and firmly believe, like we believe the sun will rise, that *if you're not happy, it's because of me.* This pressure tends to express itself more subtly than other pressures, but the message comes across loud and clear: "Do *not* be unhappy." The spouse feels the unnamed pressure, and comes to resent it.

There is the pressure to like your family. Or your friends. But liking people is just something that happens, and you can guarantee it isn't going to happen when you insist it does (Newton's Law). The problem is, your spouse has eyes to see what you *don't* see—that your uncle is a selfish prig and an alcoholic, and your friend Becky cannot hold a conversation unless it is all about her. Insisting your spouse like your family (e.g., spend every holiday with them and "be happy" about it) is a sure bet for a whopper of a fall out sooner or later.

Christian couples feel the added pressure to have a *model* marriage. To be a "witness" to our families and neighbors. Therefore nothing can ever be wrong. We've got to present a good face to the world. We feel the pressure to pray together, to have family devotions, and to love going to church. We feel the pressure to be "Christlike" in our marriages—and since none of us are even close to that level of sainthood, we feel a lot of guilt and shame. But we feel compelled to hide all that. Because after all—we are Christians.

There is the pressure a woman puts on a man to climb the corporate ladder and to keep up with the Joneses. She wants the bigger house, the nice car. There is the pressure a man puts on a woman to be beautiful and to live up to some standard he picked up watching television, or through pornography.

Or how about the pressure to "share everything." Somebody saw a movie or read a book about a couple who were so intimate they practically thought the other's thought before they even thought it. (I know, that sounds tangled; it *is* tangled.) And therefore, any private thought or mood is not allowed. Friendships with others feel threatening—"What did you do? What did you talk about?" It's relational claustrophobia.

We talked about the pressure of the "Golden Moment." Like having to make Christmas magical. Or to re-create some summer vacation memory by revisiting that very place every year. "And we have to have s'mores on the beach." But maybe your spouse doesn't like the beach. Or s'mores. Maybe this isn't even about your marriage at all; maybe it's about trying to recapture some lost moment of your childhood and everybody pays every year because it can't be done.

There is the pressure—and how bizarre is this, really—that someone love you. Of course we want to be loved. Of course it hurts when we feel we are not loved, especially by the closest person in our life. But *insisting* that someone love you is like telling a fawn you have just seen slip into the woods to "Come Back Out," or commanding a hummingbird to land on your finger and "Stay There."

And then there is the "Biggest Pressure of All"—the pressure we feel to make each other happy. After all, this marriage is supposed to make me happy—right?

Does any of this sound familiar? Does it ring true in your marriage?

It Can't Be Done

I [John] woke up earlier than I wanted to this morning. Around 4:30 A.M. After about an hour of restless turning I knew I wasn't going to fall back asleep, so I conceded to the new day, came out into the kitchen, and made a cup of tea. Yerba Mate. I sat down on the couch. This time of year it is still dark at 5:30, and I just sat there, holding the cup in my hands, letting the warmth seep into me. My soul felt like it was coming back from some distant place. Where does it wander off to at night? I have no idea. My dreams are a vague memory. Sitting cross-legged on the sofa, cradling my cup, I began to turn my thoughts toward God. It was so good to know that I had time to linger and just be with God. *What are you saying this morning, Jesus? What do I need?*

A few moments of quiet, and then I hear, *My love.*

I'm not in crisis. Yesterday was a good day. We held some pretty energetic meetings at work; it was fun. When I got home, I fixed the leaking kitchen sink—a triumph that makes a man feel mighty fine. (I tried to help Stasi relate, "Imagine you just lost five pounds today.")

After dinner I finished a book I'd been enjoying. Stasi and I are in a good place. We snuggled when we went to bed. But all that was *yesterday*. As I am regaining consciousness this morning, coming back to myself, none of that remains. My soul is needy again. Good grief—I feel like a sponge. I can take in so much in a day, almost ravenously, feel pretty good, but the next day I am dried out. Again.

This is the nature of our condition. All of us are leaky vessels. Sandy soil. When it comes to happiness, our soul is like a colander, a tire with a nail in it, our grandfather's memory. It feels like there is a homeless person inside of us, wandering around pushing a shopping cart.

This is brutal on a marriage.

We can have the best sex, kick over the nightstand sex, but as a man I want it again the next morning. That was last night. What about today? We can have the most intimate conversation, deep soul connection, but as a woman Stasi wants it again the next day.

Sometimes it is just a look in Stasi's eyes as she comes into the kitchen in the morning—*Am I okay? Are we okay?* And I think to myself, *Geez freaking Louise, we had a great night last night. It made no difference? What's it gonna take?* It can be wearying. You're not satisfied?

Let's face it—we are insatiable. We have in each of us a famished craving. An aching void. A returning hunger. If we are not aware of this, and if we don't know how to handle it, our insatiability will do a lot of damage.

Of Course You Are Disappointed

The human heart has an infinite capacity for happiness and an unending need for love, because it is created for an infinite God who is unending love. The desperate turn is when we bring the aching abyss of our hearts to one another with the hope, the plea, "Make me happy. Fill this ache." And often out of love we *do* try to make one another happy, and then we wonder why it never lasts.

It can't be done.

You will kill yourself trying.

We are broken people, with a famished craving in our hearts. We are fallen, all of us. It happened so long ago, back in the Garden of Eden, so early in our story that most of us don't even realize it happened. But the *effects* of the Fall are something we live with every day, and it would be best for both of you if you understood what it has done to the soul of a man and a woman.

Every woman now has an insatiable need for relationship, one that can never be filled. It is an ache in her soul designed to drive her to God. Men instinctively know that the bottomless well is there, and pull back. *I don't want to be engulfed by that. Besides, no matter how much I offer, it'll never be enough.* This is Eve's sorrow. This is the break in her cup. She aches for intimacy, to be known, loved, and *chosen*. And it also explains her deepest fear—abandonment.

Men face a different sort of emptiness. We are forever frustrated in our ability to conquer life. That's the "sweat of your brow . . . thorns and thistles" thing. "Cursed is the ground because of you; through painful toil you will eat of it all the days of your life. It will produce thorns and thistles for you. . . ." (Genesis 3:17–18).

A man aches for affirmation, for validation, to know that he has come through. This also explains his deepest fear—failure.

Now, take these fears, brokenness, and this famished craving, throw them together into the same house and lock the door. What ensues is the pain, disappointment, and confusion most people describe as their marriage. But what did you expect? I mean, are you really surprised?

Of course you are disappointed with your marriage.

It is not a sin to admit that. It is not a betrayal. And it need not be an earthquake. (In fact, if you cannot admit the disappointment of your marriage, you have made an idol of it. It has become "The Thing We Cannot Question.") Of course you are disappointed; your spouse is disappointed, too. How can we possibly be enough for one another?

Two broken cups cannot possibly fill one another. Happiness flows through us like water through a volleyball net.

"I keep telling him he's doing great. It doesn't seem to sink in."
"I don't know how many times I've shown her I am here for her. It's like she doesn't believe me or something."

It is so disheartening. We feel responsible for our spouse's unhappiness: *I'm not doing enough. I'm not enough. If I were a better man, a better woman, she or he would be happy. It must be me.*

Let this go on for a while and we move from guilt to resentment: *Can't you be happy with anything? It's never enough for you, is it?* How you are doing becomes the report card on me. If you are not happy, I must not be doing it right, doing enough.

It is a vicious cycle. Especially for those who are trying hard *to* love.

The good news is, of course, you aren't enough. You never, ever will be. This should come as a tremendous relief, actually. *Oh, I thought it was just us. That somehow we'd missed the class on marital happiness and now we're flunking the whole course.* Nope, it is not just you. It is everyone. Knowing this allows you to take the report card away from your spouse. How your spouse is doing is *not* the verdict on you.

Let that sink in for a moment—how your spouse is doing is not the report card on you.

Your spouse's unhappiness doesn't mean you're an "F" as a person, as a spouse. Your spouse's unhappiness—and yours—means you both have a famished craving within you that only God can meet. As this begins to come clear to you, it will be an enormous relief that you cannot possibly make your spouse happy. "Of course you are disappointed, dear. I understand completely. This isn't my fault. Go to God."

Now, we are not suggesting a swing off the other side of the cliff. We have a few friends whose deep pain in their marriage comes from the fact that their spouse is totally and utterly unreachable. "I don't need a thing from you." It has nothing to do with God. It is his or her style of relating: "I won't let you get to me." This kind of utter self-protection is the very antithesis of love.

What we are saying is simply this: You have to have some place you can turn. For comfort. For understanding. For the healing of your brokenness. For love. To offer life, you must *have* life. And you can only get this from God.

"My soul finds rest in God alone" (Psalm 62:1).

Trying to sort your way through marriage without God in your life is like trying to be gracious when you are utterly sleep-deprived. At some point, you lose your ability to be kind; you lose all perspective. As David Wilcox sings,

> *We cannot trade empty for empty*
> *We must go to the waterfall*
> *For there's a break in the cup that holds love . . .*
> *Inside us all.*

(DAVID WILCOX)

The Waterfall

And so the greatest gift you can give to your marriage is for you to develop a real relationship with Jesus Christ.

This is the kindest thing you could ever do for your spouse.

We are not simply talking about believing in God. There are many good people who believe in God, but for all practical purposes they still look to their spouse to make them happy. Simply look at their anger, their confusion, their sorrow. We're talking about a relationship where you are finding in God the life and love your soul so desperately needs. This is not something reserved for mystical saints. The love of God is real, and personal, and available. He *wants* to be this for you. It is the *reason* he gave to each of us this famished craving and a leaky cup!

A car is made to run on gasoline, and it would not run properly on anything else. Now God designed the human machine to run on Himself. He Himself is the fuel our spirits were designed to burn, or the food our spirits were designed to feed on. There is no other. That is why it is just no good asking God to make us happy in our own way. . . . God cannot give us happiness and peace apart from himself, because it is not there. There is no such thing.

(C. S. LEWIS, *Mere Christianity*)

The secret of happiness is this: God is the love you are longing for.

We live in a love story. We are created for romance and we have an insatiable capacity for it. Now, God gave us such a heart; it was one of his first gifts to us. (You have to have a heart to live in a love story.) Then he gives to us this world that is so breathtakingly beautiful. "The earth is filled with the love of the Lord" (Psalm 33:5). You see it in the fact that he made grass just firm enough that it stands up straight like a carpet, but not too firm that it hurts you when you run on it with bare feet. And he makes snow just firm enough for snowballs and sledding, but not so firm that it hurts us when it falls; it falls so softly. He makes birds and their songs just loud enough to be delightful, and he creates our ear to delight in the sound. Do you begin to see the tenderness and the love of God through all creation?

And then he gives to each of us those unique and particular things that capture our hearts, those things we loved when we were young and those things we love even still—horses, the wind, and playing an instrument or baseball. He gave you all the things that you have ever loved, and all those joys that are unique and particular to you—the puppy you got when you were seven, your favorite bike, running barefoot on the grass in the summertime in the evenings when the dew was on the grass and the day was still warm but the grass was cool. All of this is the love of God wooing you.

Some of you found the romance of God at the beach. Some of you found it on the rivers or in the meadows. Some of you found it in books. All that has ever stirred your heart, that was God romancing you. For as the Bible says, "Every good and perfect gift comes down from the Father above" (James 1:17).

Sometimes I [John] will walk out of the house in the early morning or I'll be taking the dog out in the late evening and suddenly a breeze will come and just brush my cheek. I have finally come to realize that it is God wooing me. And you know what I'll do? I'll turn my face into it. That is what he wants. He wants us to turn our faces into those things that he is bringing to woo our hearts. He wants us to turn all of that longing and all of that desire, and just give it over to him. That is how you experience the love of God.

Now we understand that this is something to be cultivated. There are many books on that. (We have written a few ourselves, including *The Sacred Romance* and *Walking with God*.) But the first and the most important thing we can do is simply pray, "God, open my eyes to your love. Give me a revelation of your love for me. I've lost it. I've lost sight of it. Lord, draw my heart back to you. Open my eyes so that I can see how you are wooing me."

Understanding how deeply a woman needs to know she is loved, that she is beautiful, that she will not be abandoned—these are the very questions she must bring to God. *Ladies, your marriage better not be the primary place you are looking for intimacy!* And knowing how deeply a man needs affirmation, that he too is loved, and that he has what it takes—this he must bring to God. *Guys, your marriage better not be the primary place you are looking for validation!*

This is the kindest thing you could ever do for the people in your life—to have somewhere you can turn, someone who loves you and understands. Some of the sweetest times I have had with God have come during some of the hardest times in our marriage.

It does not mean you don't love your spouse. It does not mean that your spouse is not important to you. It simply means that you understand you are not a well and your spouse is not a well. You are both leaky buckets in search of a well. It lifts all of that crushing expectation off of a marriage. It rescues your marriage from resignation, and then you have something whimsical and light to bring to the relationship.

Now, here is the beautiful part of our twenty-fifth wedding anniversary story. Once Stasi realized where all this ache was coming from and gave her hurting heart to God, she happily released her expectations for the day and released us all from the pressure to create the "Golden Moment." Once the anniversary was freed up, it turns out we actually had a wonderful day.

There's all sorts of joy to be found in your marriage, once you stop looking to your spouse to make you happy.

FIVE

More Than Just Roommates

The companion of an evening, and the companion for life, require very different qualifications.

—— SAMUEL RICHARDSON

Today is the twenty-fifth anniversary of our marriage. Now that the pressure has been lifted off the day, I [John] am looking forward to it. I *want* it to be rich, and beautiful. Sam—our eldest, away for his second year at college—just texted me from Los Angeles International Airport. He is on his way home for our party tonight. Flowers have arrived; decorations will soon be hung. Stasi's sister just sent us something that I think might be a birdbath; I'm guessing Stasi will understand the gift. Anyhow, preparations are in full swing.

I've pulled out the card I bought for Stasi, and I am wondering what in heaven's name do I write in it? How do you even begin to find the words to speak to twenty-five years of life together? I'm floundering a bit with what to say. I bought a blank card because I would prefer to write my own message. (Not every guy is like this. I'm a writer, for heaven's sake. So cut him some slack, ladies.) But this is almost an impossible task. I have been married to Stasi for more than half of my life. We have lived more of our years together than we have lived apart. If you take childhood out of the equation, we have lived nearly *all* of our adult years together. We have, in so many ways, grown up together.

In the early hours of this morning I was sitting here thinking: *What is it I have most enjoyed with Stasi? What is it I would say has been her greatest gift to me? What am I most grateful for?* The question helped me find my way. It drew me to the core, the real substance of our marriage—companionship. Don't get me wrong—I love passion, romance, and sexual intimacy. Eros is intoxicating. But Eros does not a marriage make. The richest part, the *daily* goodness, is companionship. Who else is always there at the end of the day, every day? Who else is with you in the dark hours of the night? Who else is by your side in joy and in sorrow? No one but your spouse even comes close to sharing your life.

There's a scene we both love in the movie *Shall We Dance?* The story is about a marriage that has not so much fallen on hard times as fallen into the doldrums of routine. The wife fears her husband might be having an affair; she hires a private detective to find out what he's up to. It turns out that he's spending his Wednesday nights taking ballroom dancing lessons! She tells the detective she no longer needs his services. He is intrigued by her devotion to her husband, and they have this parting conversation.

Wife: Why is it do you think that people get married?
Detective: Passion.
Wife: No.
Detective: That's interesting because I would have taken you for a romantic. Why then?
Wife: Because we need a witness to our lives. There's a billion people on the planet. I mean what does any one life really mean? But in a marriage, you're promising to care about everything. The good things. The bad things. The terrible things. The mundane things. All of it. All the time. Every day. You're saying, "Your life will not go unnoticed be-

cause I will notice it. Your life will not go unwitnessed because I will be your witness."

I will be your witness. I will be your companion. Through thick and thin, the good and the bad, in sickness and in health, we are in this thing together. Isn't this the essence of what God was expressing when he said, "It is not good for man to be alone" (Genesis 2:18)? But of course. Passion comes and goes like thunderstorms. Romance blossoms like night-blooming flowers. Companionship is far more steady, more day in and day out, like the presence of God. Lo, I am with you always. We promised that in our vows, didn't we? "I am here to stay."

It might not have the drama that sexual passion offers, but, "How was your day?" might be the most beautiful gift a marriage offers. Waiting to and wanting to hear the answer conveys, "Your life matters. Your life has meaning."

C. S. Lewis poses a really compelling question when he asks couples if they would rather have Eros or Companionship:

Suppose you are fortunate enough to have "fallen in love with" and married your Friend. And now suppose it possible that you were offered the choice of two futures: "Either you two will cease to be lovers but remain forever joint seekers of the same God, the same beauty, the same truth, or else, losing all that, you will retain as long as you live the raptures and ardors, all the wonder and the wild desire of Eros. Choose which you please." Which should we choose? Which choice should we not regret after we had made it?

(C. S. LEWIS, *The Four Loves*)

Hopefully, we are never forced to make this choice; may God grant us the blessing of sharing both all our lives. But, if I had to choose, without a doubt I would choose companionship (I am an older man now; in my younger days I might have chosen Eros and regretted it later). Companionship is far more the actual brick and mortar of two lives lived together. Companionship is the glue that allows a marriage to make it, not just through the hard times, but make it in the sense of finding your way to something rich together.

Belonging to Each Other

And the two shall become one. . . .

—GENESIS 2:24

In the heart of every human being lies the desire to belong. It is primordial, primeval, linked somewhere in our deep memory to our need for survival. To be the outcast is to be sentenced to death. To be shunned is the worst form of punishment. Solitary confinement is used to break prisoners. In our modern world, when we are deemed unworthy, physical gates do not bar us from the safety of our community but the gates are closed to us nonetheless.

All of us have known the cruelty of middle school cliques, high school cliques, college cliques, and ministry cliques. Some have experienced the terrifying power of psychological bullying—mean girls, ruthless boys. Did you make the team, the squad, the court? Do you fit in? How many friends are on your Facebook page? Did you get asked to the dance? Did she say yes? Is your picture in the yearbook more than once? Did you get accepted, asked, invited? *Are you in or are you out?*

Life is meant to be shared; we are supposed to feel "in." We are meant to live in community, in relationship with others. People may drive us crazy sometimes, but still we need each other. One is the loneliest number and all that. Now, some of us are born introverts— we replenish our spirits and souls best in the company of just ourselves and our God. In fact, everyone needs time alone. Regularly. But in the same way, everyone needs to be in the company of others as well, regularly.

After turning his back on society and finding his way into the Alaskan wilderness with only himself as a companion, Christopher McCandless discovered that he missed the very people he was trying to escape. He became profoundly lonely. He realized that life was not meant to be lived alone and that "happiness is only real when shared."

Isn't it true? When something really good happens, we can't wait to share it. My mother [Stasi here] passed away seven years ago, but in a moment of victory or happiness, I still think of her and want to give her a call to share the news. The same holds true with tragedy. When a crisis occurs—when the doctor calls with scary news or when our world is shaken—we need the companionship of others. We need someone who loves us, who truly cares, to come alongside of us and share in our experience. As a woman, one of the best things about being married is this: The question "Who will I go with?" is forever answered. I belong to someone; I have a mate. We are a pair, a couple, a set. We are no longer single, we are a double. If we played bridge anymore, we would be a team. We have a tennis partner, a dance partner, someone to sit next to at the table, and a date for the rest of our Friday nights. We are a couple; we belong to each other. Two really are better than one, in a host of ways.

John and I have walked through some very hard times together: the death of dear friends; the loss of long-term relationships; many hospital visits; moving cross-country three times. We have also shared some really wonderful times, too: traveling in Scotland and Ireland; speaking together at conferences; snorkeling in Mexico; realizing a lifelong dream of buying a ranch. And then there are all the "in-between times": making the boys lunches in the evening; texting each other when we are out and about; saying our bedtime prayers together for twenty-five years.

But like you, we have also seen some really lonely years in our marriage.

And to be lonely in your marriage is the loneliest feeling of all.

And the Two Shall Stay as Two

When John and I moved to Colorado, Luke had not yet been born. Sam was just over two years old and Blaine was only nine months old. I worked part time a couple of evenings a week but John was the primary breadwinner. I spent my days at home raising, nurturing, playing with, and caring for our boys. As a man, John was finding his place in the workforce—challenging himself, desiring to grow personally and professionally, as well as wanting to provide for his family. He worked hard and wanted to prove himself. After Luke came along, John went back to school to earn his master's degree in counseling. It was a great program and I was 100 percent behind him.

But he was really busy. He still worked full time, traveling the country doing conferences many weekends a year. He was given Mondays and Tuesdays off to make up for the weekends he worked. And Mondays and Tuesdays were spent at the university. On a rare day off, in much need of rest and refreshment, John would take our one car and go fishing. Spending the day on the water brought life to him; God was meeting him there. More than half of his days off were spent on the river. By himself or with a friend. Not with me. Not with our sons.

It was common for him to be gone every day of the week for three or four weeks at a time. The longest stretch we went was seven weeks in a row of John being away from home every single day. The pattern went on for two years. Can I mention again how young our children were?

Are any of you women reading this irritated with him yet?

My best friend sure was.

Somehow in my heart I knew God was moving in my husband. I understood I had to let him go and not demand he stay home. When he was home, John was completely present. He engaged with our sons deeply, profoundly. They had then and they have now a rare and wonderful relationship. But those were hard years. For both of us. I felt that John was running away from me.

I was asked so many times by others, *"When is it your turn?"*

Countless times, well-meaning friends and family would speak of John with irritation and anger. I was even encouraged once to divorce him. None of it was helpful. None of it.

Part of the problem at the time was the major issues in our marriage that needed addressing. My insecurity as a woman made me feel that I wasn't worth fighting for or standing up for. Somewhere along the road I had lost my sense of self. I thought John was fabulous; I didn't think too highly of me. John had and still has strong opinions, distinct likes, and distinct dislikes (he is incredibly hard to buy a present for). I had melted into not knowing who I was, what I liked, or what I wanted. If a marriage means the two become one, in my marriage the two became John. And that is not what God had in mind.

The goal of marriage being oneness doesn't mean the two become one person. It means the two separately become better people. Together. As Candice Bergen said: "I used to believe that marriage would diminish me, reduce my options. That you had to be someone less to live with someone else, when, of course, you have to be someone more." But John and I were far apart in every way. Those were hard and lonely years.

Looking back I [John] see it more clearly now, why Stasi felt abandoned. Trying to make my way in the world, dogged by all those fears that "I am on my own," pushing myself hard, I was gone an awful lot. Many young men feel this pressure, this compulsion to slay the wolf and the bear, to stake a claim. But in spite of those very real battles, the reality was I ran away. We lived very separate lives.

But there is more to the story.

For the first ten years of our marriage Stasi struggled with an eating disorder and with depression. To be honest, it felt like she had left the building. The alive, passionate, and opinionated woman that I had married was all but gone. Only, she was still there, which was crazy-making. How can you be present to someone who isn't present? I'm not making excuses, simply filling in some of the story.

There are always "reasons" behind the choices that cause us to end up living in different worlds. The details may vary, but the story is fairly common. Despite our vows, our hopes and dreams, most couples end up living separate lives.

When the two of you spend time apart, what are the real reasons behind that? What typically happens is that both the man and woman get busy. You go to work; you come home exhausted. If you have children, they get what is left of you before bedtime. If you are successful in work or in ministry, it eats you alive. If you are barely surviving, it devours your hope and energy along with your time. Then we all look for a little something to refill our cups, doing what we enjoy or just vegging out in front of the television. And our spouse gets the dregs. We end up feeling like "two separate careerists in the same bed," as Wendell Berry described it.

Picture the classic images from the movie *Citizen Kane* depicting the slow but inevitable dissolution of the marriage of Charles Foster Kane and his wife. The young couple begin their domestic life at a tiny table in the kitchen, sharing meals close together and very much in love. (We did the same, eating off a card table loaned to us by Stasi's mother.) Over time—as the tyranny of success creeps in—the Kanes' table grows in size, and we watch the couple grow farther apart. The final scene shows Kane and his wife at a massive dining room table the size of a hockey rink, seated at the far ends, taking their meals in separate worlds. By the time it occurs, their divorce is merely a formality.

We walked to the brink of divorce (again), in our tenth year of marriage, when we were about as distant as two lives can get. We both looked over that precipice, and we didn't like what we saw. By the grace of God—and his grace is always what's behind a good marriage—we began to make choices to move toward one another.

It's the Choices We Make

Sitting around the dining table as a family last New Year's Eve (we have a round table now, to keep everyone close and in the conversation), John asked a question. "What was one of your best moments in the past year?" The question did not come as a surprise to me (we do this every New Year's Eve), but when it came back around to John, his answer did. He spoke of a time during the summer when he and I had ridden horses together on our ranch, just the two of us meandering through the aspens and the sage, taking in the mountain views. How rich, wonderful, and epic it had been.

It thrilled my heart to hear that my husband's favorite moment of his whole year was a certain moment spent with me. It also provoked something. That time riding with John had been my last good experience on a horse. A month later he'd had that bad fall that broke his wrists, and I'd been thrown twice. I wasn't liking horses so much anymore. Riding them wasn't too appealing. They scared me. But it was my husband's *favorite* experience of a time spent with me. It mattered to his heart. And his heart is something worth fighting for.

It took me a while to get up the courage, but I found a woman who does horse therapy to help me get over my fear. What happened in that arena with her and those three therapy horses in a little over an hour was miraculous really. God came. And he took my fear. And I have gotten back in the saddle again. For my husband. For both of us really. To be able to share with him moments that are glorious and minister to his heart builds beauty into our marriage and deepens our friendship. And boy do I love that!

So here is a simple question to ask yourself: What do you do simply because your spouse wants to do it?

During the month of March, I [John] am glued to the television watching college basketball. During last year's March Madness, Stasi came into the room one Saturday afternoon and said she would like to go furniture shopping. With me. I wanted to watch the Georgetown game; she wanted my help finding a few things for the house. Here is where the rubber meets the road; this is where companionship gets lived out. Guys, what would you typically do? A choice is going to be made, however else you might cloak it. As proof that the Holy Spirit really can change a person, I humbly confess that I chose to go shopping. Really. (Okay, I admit, it wasn't one of the Final Four games.)

There was a particular store Stasi wanted to visit; it is one of her favorites. The moment I walked in the door I was reeling; the place was an assault on the senses. There was not one free inch of open space on the walls, the shelves, or the floors. The place was bursting with frou-frou, tchotchkes, lacey this, antique that. My male survival instincts kicked in: Run! Get me out of this jungle! Yet another choice had to be made: I will stay engaged; I will not flee. I will not pout in order to get Stasi to cut this short.

I ignored the scented candles and remained by her side, interested and engaged.

We talked about which picture we liked better for the bedroom. We looked through catalogs and ordered a piece of furniture. We spent as much time there as Stasi wanted to spend. (Oh! Look at this! Isn't this darling!)

I knew that choosing to stay present in that moment with her was the way to say, "I love you. I want to be with you. What matters to you matters to me." This is crucial, guys: It is not simply that you participate, but how you enter in. Stasi wanted my thoughts, my opinions, and she wanted to share hers with me.

It was a fun afternoon. Truly it was.

A Word of Caution

Before we say more about finding genuine companionship with one another, let us put this in context. *Both of you need other friends.*

Women need women friends and men need men friends. Far too often, especially in the early years, a couple will retreat into their bower—behind "the shining barrier" as the author Sheldon Vanauken called it—pulling away from even lifelong friends. This is foolish. You need the camaraderie of friends outside the marriage. We think a woman needs friends even more than her husband, because a woman's relational needs are more vast than a man's. Guys can be happy watching the game once a week with some buddies. Women need to *talk*. Daily.

So fellas, I have always made it my mission, whenever we have moved to a new city, to do everything I could to help Stasi find some girlfriends. Every time she has ever asked to go out and do something with the girls, I have *always* said yes.

And women, you can't pin your need for friendship on your husband. (Many women try to.) There are too many things you enjoy that he simply won't. Once they get married, many women expect their husband to become their best and primary friend. This is especially true if they have moved to another city (or moved often, as military wives must do). It puts a pressure on him that he will come to resent.

And men, there is nothing in your marriage that can provide you what masculine fellowship can provide. Do not give this up thinking that now you are married you don't need it or that you must stay home. You need other men friends *so that* you can be a better husband and father.

Here is the key: We want to be able to offer something to our spouses out of a full heart, *and not merely bring them our need.* Your friendships help you to return home with something to give.

As Thomas à Kempis said, "Without a friend thou canst not well live; and if Jesus be not above all a friend to thee, thou wilt be sad and desolate." In all seasons of life, let us remember that there is no friend like Jesus, so intimate, so unfailing, and we must find friendship with him above all else. Wherever we are, he is always there, the truest and most faithful companion you could ever have.

Recovering Genuine Companionship

John has a circle of things he loves to do. It includes fly-fishing, rock climbing, working on cars, hunting, reading, smoking cigars, and just about anything with adventure in it. I have a circle of things I love to do. It encompasses going to movies, working in and enjoying my garden, talking, taking walks, worshipping, and reading novels. *Oh, dear. Hopefully, somewhere, we can find some overlap.*

I am also the mother of three sons. I live in a household of men. I love them passionately but it can be lonely at times being the only woman around. Do some of you feel that way too? It isn't easy to find places to connect with them and to share in their lives. I don't play Xbox. I'm not a hunter. I'm not a rock climbing, mountain biking, backpacking, snowboarding teenager. Often I don't even understand them. I long for real relationships with them and have been praying for ways to connect.

And John just gave me a Ping-Pong table for Christmas. Ladies, I know what you are thinking—*doghouse gift; what a miss*! But John knew what he was doing. My family had a Ping-Pong table while I was growing up and I spent hours playing with my brother and with my dad. Those are sweet memories for me, times of real connection with my family. The present of a Ping-Pong table was an invitation to connect. Now I am playing with my sons and my husband. Team games. Single games. It doesn't matter games, because we are spending time together doing something we all enjoy. *Big sigh.* Yay!

I also love water. I love being near it, on it, and in it. Pools, ponds, lakes, rivers, streams, oceans, and even bathtubs! All of it. Diving in, putting my head under, swimming as deeply as I can breathes life into me. I'm happy sitting next to a beautiful mountain lake; I am happier paddling a canoe on top of it, but happier still diving into it. We have found ways to share our love of water. First, John introduced me to canoes, those wobbly precarious silent crafts that can explore shallow channels and mysterious inlets. How many adventures we have had paddling around lakes, bays, and rivers! He got me into my first kayak; I was so close to the water I was sitting in it but somehow still remained dry. It was while we were kayaking as a family that we came so breathlessly close to a humpback whale; I felt I'd crossed back into Eden.

Over the years we have found other ways to build companionship.

We love to travel. We love going out for Chinese food. We share with each other movies that we like, or something from a book that has stirred us. John loves the wilderness; we found a way to enjoy it together using lodges. In this way we can spend a day out on the trail, but at night I get a shower and a bed!

And, we still enjoy many of our loves alone, or with other friends.

There is no need to feel jealous that your spouse loves to do things without you. There is simply no way you can be everything to each other; your hearts are too vast and your interests are too diverse for you to "be one in everything." It would be weird if it were otherwise. And of course you want your spouse to have a "full cup," to be filled and happy and well; they will be so much easier to live with. And they won't be looking to you to make them happy. So good grief, do not fight their enjoyment of other things or other people! Sometimes I [Stasi] would feel that I was in competition with John's close friends and other interests. How freeing to come to understand that that was not the case. The place I hold in John's heart is not up for grabs. (But John had to reassure me this was so, and God needed to move in my heart so I could believe it.)

There is an ebb and flow to the companionship of a marriage. During hunting season, I don't expect to see John much. But afterward, I *do* expect him to come home and reengage with me! There are seasons when the two of us are "connecting" well and seasons when we aren't. What you want to do is create an environment where over time and with intentionality, you are nurturing companionship. Every day is unrealistic; once a month isn't often enough. Somewhere in between.

This can feel a little awkward if it has been a while since the two of you spent time together. Initiate anyway, and don't be put off if your first few efforts aren't warmly received. A friend tried to get her husband to enjoy bubble baths; *that* was a miss. Watching *American Idol* might be a miss. Bass fishing might be a miss. But you are going to have to find some meeting place together. Tennis. Beachcombing. Vietnamese food. A favorite TV show. Scrabble. Square dancing. Do you ever read together? (One suggestion: Maybe you two could read this book together and talk about it chapter by chapter.)

Maybe you should just ask your spouse what they'd like to do. Our suggestion is to explore this together. Find those intersections of life that you each enjoy and both can share.

Can It Really Happen?

Last summer our son Sam was asking a number of people a question. He was doing a sort of personal survey: "Do you believe there is one person in the world for you to marry, or do you believe that you could marry a handful of different people and be happy with them?"

There was an underlying fear to this, a lurking deeper question, which if put into words would go something like this: "Is there one perfect mate for me out there? Can I miss the will of God and ruin my life by marrying the wrong person?"

What do you think?

We believe the answer to his first question—the "either/or" question—is yes and yes. We believe the answer to his unasked deeper question is no.

God knows who you are going to marry. When you *do* marry that person, your spouse becomes the one person you were *supposed to* marry. Yes, people make mistakes. All the time. Sometimes people marry the wrong person. We have had good friends make this heart-wrenching mistake and realize it early into their marriage. But it was not a death sentence, not on their life *or* on their marriage. It really is true "that in all things God works for the good of those who love Him, who have been called according to his purpose" (Romans 8:28).

One friend I [Stasi] love deeply was considering marriage. I warned her that I thought she was making a bad decision. I laid out my reasons why I thought so. They were valid. But she was certain and went ahead with the marriage. (And by the way, once married, I became a strong ally *for* the marriage and for the man.) She called me within the year to say that I had been right; she had made a mistake.

But then she said—and this shows the character of my friend—
that she was committed to loving this man *unto* the man God
wanted him to become while allowing God *to transform her* into becoming the best suited wife for him. They have been married for
over twenty years now. Yes, there have been hard times. The disappointments have driven her to a deeper intimacy with God. And
she loves her husband well. They have a good marriage.

There is no such thing as the perfect spouse; that is the fantasy
weirdness of *The Stepford Wives.* The best husband for you is the husband you have; the best wife for you is the wife you have. Consider
Nathalia Crane's lines in light of your present circumstances,

> *You cannot choose your battlefield*
> *God does that for you;*
> *But you can plant a standard*
> *Where a standard never flew.*

(NATHALIA CRANE)

Here you are—make your stand. This is the man or woman
whose heart you have been entrusted with. You really have no idea
what depths of companionship are available until you venture into
those waters, and hang in there for many years. Besides, your own
transformation is barely under way. Who knows all that God has in
store for the both of you? We would say that at twenty-five years
we are just beginning to understand.

SIX

How to Have a Really Good Fight

The most dangerous food is wedding cake.

—— JAMES THURBER

Stasi is really bugging me this morning.

I can't name it; I don't even know why. She's just bugging me, that's all. I'm irritated with her—or rather, what it feels like is simply that *she's irritating*. And truth be told, she doesn't seem that happy to see me, either. I don't get it. We just had a very romantic weekend together.

The redemption of our twenty-fifth wedding anniversary went like this: First, we did end up having a party—not the gala event of the elusive Golden Moment, but an intimate gathering at our home, which was even better. Champagne, a lovely cake, loving toasts, joy. It was beautiful. The next morning we slipped away to Santa Fe for three days. There is a lot to tell from that adventure, but let me jump to the best moment. It is our second evening. We're going to a restaurant recommended by some friends, and rated tops in a city known for great restaurants. Anticipation is high. That ancient yearning for Eden is stirring in our hearts. *This might be really good.*

Now, you recall the backstory—how four years ago, while playing a board game, Josh Groban's "When You Say You Love Me" comes on over the stereo and Stasi stops playing to make the announcement, "I want to dance to this at our twenty-fifth." In classic guy fashion, I totally forgot about it. I think something in me cringed at the thought of dancing a slow, romantic dance, gazing into each other's eyes as fifty of our family and friends surrounded us like voyeurs. So, let's just say I didn't make a strong mental note of it. By the time our anniversary came around, it was totally gone. I'm sad to say, I forgot all about the song.

Anyhow, it is a little tense getting to the restaurant. One-way streets, I can't navigate my pickup truck into the tiny parking spots, and tension is mounting. The evening feels fragile; joy feels fragile, like Cinderella's slipper. It feels like we are going to miss the ball. We come into the restaurant and—it is lovely. Linen tablecloths, crystal wineglasses, and a fire in the adobe fireplace. Really romantic. The aromas wafting from the kitchen are absolutely heavenly. The waiter brings our drinks and steps away for a moment. We both take a deep breath, and let out a long sigh. We lift our wineglasses for a toast, and at this moment we become aware of the music that is playing.

Josh Groban is singing "When You Say You Love Me."

We smile.

The evening becomes transcendent. We're lifted into the Love Story.

It is altogether beautiful. Our waiter confides that he loves our books, and that is fun. We let him in on our celebration. The food is exquisite. Best of all, we are ourselves. The veil is lifted, the pressure of life held at bay. We are simply ourselves, and we really do enjoy each other. It is good to be reminded of that. As dinner lingers on, each course is better than the one before. I don't recall what they named our dessert, but it should have been called chocolate orgasm. At the close of the evening I ask for the bill, and our waiter says that it has already been paid for by our friends. We are speechless and moved to tears. Later we wander the romantic grounds of our hotel, holding hands. Then we retire to our room and—well, let's just say it was a passionate finale.

But now . . . I'm irritated, she's certain I'm disappointed (back to our old wounds), and everything we just enjoyed is slipping away. What the heck is going on? Why does it always seem that any movement toward love or romance or redemption, any step toward joy, is just waiting to be tripped up?

You Have an Enemy

Back to the drama in the Garden of Eden.

Remember now, God gave us this story of the first marriage to help us get our bearings. It provides some very essential categories for navigating *our* marriages—like how gender is so fundamental to our identity, and how we were made for Paradise. How mankind fell and what that Fall did to our lives *as* men and women. And it also makes something else absolutely and utterly clear—we have an enemy.

Now there's a thought.

I mean, we all feel from time to time that we have an enemy, but who would we say that is? Our spouse—right? Sometimes you just walk into the room and *see* them and they feel like the enemy. "One day out of three," a friend cynically said to me.

But your spouse is not the enemy. There is another.

We confessed earlier in the book our naïve view of the story when we got married. We thought the plot was, "Love God. Love each other. And everything will work out!" Our naïveté nearly cost us our marriage. We learned the hard way (do any of us ever really learn any other way?) that there is a whole lot more going on here. We had to face our brokenness. That was a shock. We had to confront our style of relating. That was humbling. We needed to learn that this is a far more dangerous story than we thought, that there is so much at stake. And maybe the biggest eye-opener of all—*we learned we had an enemy.*

No one explained that to us in our early years, or if they did, we weren't paying attention. But this is a given in Scripture. Toward the end of his life the seasoned old Saint Peter pens a word of warning to the followers of Christ:

> *Be self-controlled and alert. Your enemy the devil prowls around like a roaring lion looking for someone to devour. Resist him, standing firm in the faith, because you know that your brothers throughout the world are undergoing the same kind of sufferings.*

(I PETER 5:8)

He assumes that every single one of us ("your brothers throughout the world") are under assault by a very real enemy, whom he portrays as a ravenous lion, stalking us, just waiting for the first chance to devour. Not merely "tempt." Devour. If you have seen the movie *The Ghost and the Darkness,* you have some idea. It was a sobering description Peter's readers would have *taken* soberly, living as they did in lion country. It might help us moderns to think of Satan as a terrorist—cunning, dangerous, obsessed—looking to destroy whatever he can in your life, with no regard to the rules of fair play.

We hear it, but we don't seem to hear it.

I'm thinking of the story of an affair. Leslie came to my office in tears—her husband had left her. "I should have seen it coming." I hold my tongue, because she's sobbing. But we *all* saw it coming. Where was he going on all those "trips"? He didn't travel for work. Everyone knew that. Then folks started seeing him with this gal in town. Friends tried to intervene; we tried to help her see. But Leslie didn't see; she didn't *want* to see. There was lipstick on his neck. He claimed it was the dental hygienist and that somehow it rubbed off when she was doing his teeth! I kid you not. And Leslie *believed* him! Can you believe it? When he finally walked out for good, most of us wanted to say, "Well what did you expect? You ignored every warning in the book."

But we are just as taken in. We don't live like our marriage has an enemy. We ignore the lipstick. Satan is respected in the Bible as a very active threat, but few people actually *live* like it. Seriously, how many couples do you know that recognize what Satan is doing in their lives and actually pray against it on a daily basis? Weekly? Monthly? When it comes to the enemy, we are all Leslie.

You have an enemy. Your marriage has an enemy.

Believe it or not, this is very good news.

Because the epiphany that follows is this—your spouse is not the enemy. He is not the enemy. She is not the enemy. Really.

"Sometimes we have to say that to each other, when things are getting heated," my friend Dan confessed. "I have to tell her, 'I am not the enemy. You are not the enemy.' Because it sure can feel that way."

It sure can. For years Stasi and I lived with this constant feeling of accusation in our marriage. She "felt" accused by me, and I "felt" accused by her. What a relief it was to discover that these feelings of accusation were not actually ours; they were coming from him who is called "the Accuser" (Revelation 12:10).

Dear friends, if this is *not* a category you think in, you will not understand your life and you will surely not understand what is happening in your marriage. If this is not an assumption you use to interpret daily thoughts, emotions, and events, you will be as bamboozled as dear Leslie. Pressed to choose our "top three things that would most help your marriage," we would come down to this list:

1. Find life in God.
2. Deal with your brokenness.
3. Learn to shut down the spiritual attacks
   that come against your marriage.

Practice this and nothing else, and you will be *amazed* at the freedom, love, and joy that will begin to flow.

The Agreements We Make

A friend was describing to us the battle on a typical morning in his house. (It might be any married household.) He is running late, and he is not in a frame of mind for conversation. But his wife has got a few things she needs to run by him. "Honey, what do you think we ought to send the kids for Christmas?" He tries a quick dodge. "I dunno, sweetheart. Just send them what we did last year." He keeps moving toward the door, and as he grabs the car keys he gives them an extra shake, for effect. (*Jingle, jingle, gotta go.*) She ignores the movement and the keys. "What about your mom? Maybe we ought to have her down for Thanksgiving. You know she didn't come last year. . . ." *Oh my God,* he thinks, *she's got a whole list.* By now, the internal commentary running in his head has drowned his wife out, ". . . and would you call the plumbers?" *She's nagging me. I hate it when she does that.*

"Okay, Sweetie. Gotta go," and with that he jumps out the front door, as if his house was on fire. At least, that is the relief he feels upon his escape. But the climax of the scene is yet to be played.

As he pulls out of the driveway, he is irritated. He gives way to the irritation, allows himself to feel irritated, and it feels good, in a sick sort of way. Like picking a scab. *I hate it when she does that.* Now what he doesn't realize is that he is being baited. There is another Presence in the car, egging all this on. An external source of provocation, but it feels so linked to real events (what just happened in the kitchen) that he doesn't see it for what it is. *She's always nagging me. She's such a nag.* It feels so justified. He is making an agreement. *It's always been like this. It will never change.* Irritation becomes cynicism; cynicism becomes resignation. He has taken the bait. The marriage has received a hairline crack. Something in the essential union of their love is, for the time being, darkened.

This sort of thing happens all the time.

Now, this might just peter out; it might not be a big deal. The day goes on, he runs into far bigger irritations at work, and by the time he gets home it is water under the bridge. But those agreements linger, like tiny cracks in the structure. They might go away over time, but more often than not they become the beginnings of deeper fissures. Little cracks don't matter much in your sidewalk, but in other places they matter a great deal—like airplane wings, for instance, or the Hoover Dam. Places that will come under immense pressure. Like marriage.

A neighbor confided in me one day that he believed he married the wrong woman. "I realized it on my wedding day."

"Really," I said. "How?"

"It just came to me. 'I made a terrible mistake. I married the wrong person.'"

I asked him if it ever occurred to him that it wasn't an epiphany from God, not even a moment of personal clarity, but a suggestion from the pit of hell.

He looked at me with absolute incomprehension, like a frog looks at you. He had swallowed the bait—hook, line, and sinker. And it destroyed his marriage. They had about fifteen years of shared disappointment, during which time he had mostly checked out. After all, he "married the wrong woman."

They divorced last year.

Deal with the Devil

We want to be as clear as possible what we mean by an "agreement."

Satan is a liar, "the father of lies" (John 8:44), so utterly convincing he deceived a glorious man and woman to betray God, whom they walked with every day. I think we tend to dismiss Adam and Eve as the idiots who got us all into this mess in the first place. But they had not yet sinned; they had experienced no wounding; they were man and woman in their glory. And they were deceived. It ought to give us all a healthy respect for what the enemy is capable of.

Even the best of us can be taken in.

Now, what this father of lies does is put his "spin" on a situation. It typically comes as a "thought" or a "feeling." *She doesn't really love you. He'll never change. She's always doing that.* (By the way, when the word "always" is part of the equation, you know you are well into an agreement.) Think of Iago whispering his lies about Desdemona to Othello in Shakespeare's *Othello*; think of Wormtongue spinning his web around Eowyn in Tolkien's *The Two Towers*. In every fairy tale, the enemy tries to pit the boy and girl against each other.

What Satan is hoping to secure from us is an "agreement," a very subtle but momentous shift in us, where we *believe* the spin, we *go with* the feeling, and we *accept* as reality the deception he is present-ing. (It always *feels* so true.) *Just settle for what you have got. Don't risk being hurt again.* Once we buy in to the lie and make the agreement, we come under the spell and come under the influence of *that* inter-pretation of events. Then it pretty much plays itself out; it becomes self-fulfilling. These agreements begin to define the relationship. They certainly color the way we experience one another. It can be devastating to just let this stuff roll on unchecked and unchal-lenged. Look what happened to Adam and Eve.

"It breaks my heart," our friend Lori said, "to realize that I've been a Christian for thirty years, and only now am I understanding this category of 'the enemy,' how he's trying to take me down." Better now than never.

The first thing we want you to do is recognize what is happening as the enemy presents an agreement, and give it no quarter. Fight it, resist it, and send it packing to the outer reaches of hell. Recognize what is at stake here.

The kingdom teeters on the hundred small choices we make every day.

Now, many of these agreements are already deeply rooted in our lives. Some of them are so historic and familiar we barely even rec-ognize them. So, how do we acknowledge them?

Well (this will be an absolute epiphany), ask Jesus:

"Lord, what are the agreements I have been making about my
 marriage?"

"What are the agreements that I have been making about
 love?"

"What are the agreements I have been making about my
 spouse?"

To have Christ reveal those things to you will be absolutely mind-
blowing.

I [John] was giving a lecture to a group of couples not long ago,
and brought them to this exercise—to ask God to reveal the agreements they had been making in their marriage. We took a moment
to pray, and listen to what God might want to reveal. I decided to
give it a go myself, not really expecting to hear much, because after
all we have a great marriage. I don't know if it was the Lord, or just
my own soul answering, but immediately the sentence came: *It's too
much work.*

I felt like I just bit down on a good bit of foil right on top of a filling. The shudder went to my toes. Dear Lord, how long have I been
making that agreement? It felt familiar; it put words to an inner condition that felt nearly as old as our marriage. Yet these agreements
can linger under the surface for decades, until something brings
them up.

You can find the weight of any matter, find its meaning in the
Larger Story simply by asking yourself, *What is the effect of embracing
this thought? What would be lost?*

I asked myself, *What's been the effect of making that agreement?* I
saw it, saw how I shift into autopilot, push the little internal
button that says, "Cruise Control." I duck the major issues, hope
for a cordial détente. I lose my desire for something more with
Stasi. I surrender my marriage on one little suggestion. The effect
is horrible.

What are some of the agreements you recognize in your life? Let
me suggest a few:

It's just not going to get any better.

Don't rock the boat; settle for what you've got.

It's not worth the effort; don't give it one more try.

Never let anyone hurt you again.

I'm just not going to trust her/him anymore.

You do your thing and I'll do mine.

I shouldn't have married him/her.

I'd be happier with someone else.

Any of those sound familiar?

Now, as Christ reveals agreements to you, what you need to do is *break them*. You must renounce them.

Jesus, forgive me for giving place to this in my heart. I reject this agreement. I renounce it. I break agreement with—[fill in the blank, what is it?]. I break this agreement and I ask for your light and I ask for your love to come into these very places. Shine your light here. Bring me back to what is true. Bring your love into this place, Lord. In Jesus' name I pray. Amen.

If you will begin to practice this, simply asking Christ what agreements you have made, and then breaking those agreements, you will be amazed at the relief you will experience. It lets so much daylight in, like throwing the windows open and suddenly having sunshine and fresh air pour into the room. Picture Dorothy, the Cowardly Lion, the Tin Man, and the Scarecrow from *The Wizard of Oz*—we're out of the woods, we're out of the dark, we're out of the night!

A United Front

Now, we wish the enemy's work ended with agreements. But you know it doesn't. That is just the first pass, the first swipe he takes at the two of you. This demented lion-turned-psycho-killer seeks to *devour.* Or, as Jesus warned, to steal, kill, destroy (John 10:10). It is not a pretty picture. And haven't we all seen it happen more than once in the lives of the people we love? Things can get a lot rougher than merely resisting agreements.

Why is it that over the past two years, every time a dear friend of ours sets out to lend his assistance on a church trip overseas (simply to play what many would see as a "background role") his wife comes down with a terrible infection in her colon? An infection the doctors still do not understand, cannot diagnose, and cannot help to relieve? Is that coincidence? Why is it that every time Mary tries to recover sexual intimacy with her husband (something they have surrendered over the years), she has nightmares about being assaulted?

Why is it that every time Janet and Dave try to pray together, their boys get into a rip-roaring fight, and somebody gets hurt? Why is it that when Steven begins to make some headway at work, his wife, Becky, spirals into one of her depressions and remains in that dark place for some time? For that matter, why did we lose a huge chunk of this very chapter as we were writing this book? The file simply disappeared. Irrecoverable. Coincidence?

Stop for a moment, right now, and think about what is hard in your marriage. How have you been *interpreting* that? Have you blamed your spouse? Yourself? Have you just accepted it with resignation? What about Satan? Have you considered his part in it?

The more we seek to make our marriage what it was meant to be and the more we seek to play our roles in the Larger Story of God, the more intense the opposition becomes. It is a fact of life, though the opposition continues to surprise and dismay the people of God who ought to know better.

How do we handle this?

First, maintain a united front. When Satan succeeded in deceiving Adam and Eve, the first thing that fractured was their relationship with God; they withdrew from God. The very next fracture was in their marriage; they withdrew from one another. Certainly this was his intent all along. Divide and conquer. It's the oldest trick in the book. Over the centuries Satan has gotten the Church to turn its guns against itself, while he seizes the world by the back of the neck and drags it to hell.

We must not let it happen.

One of the great secrets of the Kingdom of God is the power of united prayer:

> *I tell you the truth, whatever you bind on earth will be bound in heaven, and whatever you loose on earth will be loosed in heaven. Again, I tell you that if two of you on earth agree about anything you ask for, it will be done for you by my Father in heaven.*
>
> (MATTHEW 18:19)

This is all the more true if the two united are husband and wife.

Remember, in the spiritual realm, you are seen as one. When husband and wife stand together, the demons shudder.

Remember also that Adam and Eve were given authority over the earth (". . . and let them rule" [Genesis 1:26]). So the two of you exercise authority over your "realm," your little kingdom—that includes your marriage, your home, and your children among many other things. In fact, God has raised you to a *higher* position of authority than Adam and Eve held. After Christ paid for the sins of mankind through his own blood (by which he also disarmed the claims of the enemy against us), he rose from the dead. God the Father then gave to him all authority in heaven *and on earth* (Matthew 28:18). Christ won back what Adam and Eve surrendered.

And then, God included you in the authority of Jesus Christ. "And God raised us up with Christ and seated us with him in the heavenly realms in Christ Jesus" (Ephesians 2:6). So when husband and wife stand together, they wield a great deal of power and authority.

The enemy knows this better than we, and that is why whatever form his assault is taking, you will *not* feel like praying about it together. You will suddenly feel irritated at each other. You will bow in prayer and suddenly you'll notice that he breathes heavily through his nose and it will bug the livin' daylights out of you and completely take you out of the prayer time. Or, one of you will simply want to "talk about it," which is not the same as praying about it; quite often this is a ruse of the enemy to prevent you from praying about it. It will feel hopeless; it will feel silly. Do it anyway. For if you will stand together in prayer, you *will* see results. You will have already won the first battle—you maintained a united front.

Just last night, Stasi and I were trying to navigate some difficult times with one of our sons. It was a tough conversation for the three of us; I knew we were in a battle for his heart. But the entire time I wanted to get mad at him, and also at Stasi. Later, in our bedroom, I wanted so badly to critique the way she handled the conversation. The enemy wanted me to take all my frustration with our son and turn it on Stasi. (You have probably experienced this, too—the person you are mad at *isn't* there so you let it fly on the person who *is* there.) My "anger" would have hurt her and divided us. I knew I was being baited. I knew—though I did not feel so in the moment—that Stasi is my ally in this. I had to fight hard not to give way to the enemy and let him divide us.

Now we understand that some of you are in marriages in which your spouse is not an ally at this time, neither God's ally nor yours. Let this Scripture be a word of hope to you:

If any brother has a wife who is not a believer and she is willing to live with him, he must not divorce her. And if a woman has a husband who is not a believer and he is willing to live with her, she must not divorce him. For the unbelieving husband has been sanctified through his wife, and the unbelieving wife has been sanctified through her believing husband. Otherwise your children would be unclean, but as it is, they are holy.

(1 CORINTHIANS 7:12–14)

This passage makes it clear that even when only one spouse is walking with God, it has a *powerful* effect upon the husband or the wife, and upon their household. Your prayers are still very effective.

Fighting for Each Other

Ken and Macey went at it for an hour and a half in the bathroom.

Not a fight, at least not what you'd think of as a fight—though without this understanding of an enemy it sure *would* have been a fight.

The background goes like this: Macey was sexually abused as a little girl. The enemy knows this, of course—just as he knows your story, knows where you are vulnerable, he has piled upon those wounds loads of self-hatred and abandonment. For most of her life she has had to fight agreements around self-hatred and fear of abandonment. Ken has struggled with an addiction to pornography, introduced to him on the playground at school when he was eight years old. It is a thirty-year-old addiction, which Macey is only partially aware of.

Whenever Macey discovers on their home computer a website Ken forgot to hide, she is immediately slammed with self-hatred. This takes the form of self-rejection and thoughts such as, *See— you are not enough for him. . . . He doesn't find you attractive.* And also abandonment, in the form of *One day he'll leave you. He's already half-gone now.* This has caused her to pull away from Ken, which the enemy then uses against him to lure him deeper into a world of fantasy sexual satisfaction. Which of course brings him shame and self-contempt, which in turn causes him to pull away from Macey.

Do you see how diabolical it all is? How far back the destruction of their marriage began, when they were both so young?

But they love each other, and they want to fight through this to recover all they can.

So, they are heading into a function of some sort, both of them getting dressed in the upstairs bathroom. Of course, Macey doesn't want to be seen by Ken as she gets dressed (which the enemy uses against him with feelings of rejection, which only raise all the disappointment about their sexual isolation). This is what he is feeling as he shaves and she dresses in the closet. She comes out and asks, "How do I look?"

Now the whole thing is booby-trapped.

He wants to say, "How come you always hide from me?" and she is feeling really vulnerable at this moment simply asking him how she looks. One wrong move and this blows up. But they are both learning they have an enemy and the enemy is not each other. So Ken pushes past what he is feeling and says, "You look great!" Would that were enough. But Macey is under loads of self-hatred and says, "No, I don't—I look stupid." On most days this would shut down the conversation, but Ken moves toward her. "Sweetheart, that sounds like an agreement."

It would take too long to record the next hour and twenty minutes, but here is what happened: Macey made the choice to stay present and not give way to the self-hatred long enough to let Ken pray for her. "In the name of Jesus I command this self-hatred to leave my wife and leave my home." That lifted the attack enough for Macey to break the agreement for herself. "I renounce the place I have given self-hatred in my life, every agreement I have ever given to it." As she prayed to break the agreements, she could feel the cloud lifting.

But now she is feeling afraid that Ken will see her as a burden. (*He's always having to pray for me.*) That's the fear of abandonment trying to sabotage her rescue. Ken is getting hammered with feelings of irritation (the spirit of self-hatred turning against him to get him to stop fighting for her). She has got to stay present and so does he. Only love can do this. They pray through several rounds of breaking agreements, ". . . and we bring the full work of Jesus Christ against the spirits of self-hatred and abandonment." When this stuff has had a long hold over a person, it usually takes a few rounds of prayer to get it to yield. But it does yield.

Now is the vulnerable moment. The attack has lifted, Macey is doing really well and feeling the intimacy that having her husband fight for her brings. She actually wants to make love to him, but she is not sure if he is even interested by now. She takes the huge risk of moving toward him. "Thank you, sweetheart," as she gives him a full body embrace.

The enemy tries one more angle. Ken is exhausted from the prayer, and he is getting hit with his own battles. (*You don't deserve to have sex with her because of the porn.*) He does the right thing. "Hon, I'm getting hit now. Can we pray for me?" She asks what about. If he were to say, "The whole porn thing," it could take her out because she has just tried to offer herself and she thinks what he means is *I'm not interested.* But what he says is, "I'm just feeling a lot of shame right now." So together they pray again, this time for Ken, ". . . and we bring the Cross and blood of Jesus Christ against all shame."

Finally they are both tender and vulnerable, naked in a wonderful way. One last choice has to be made. She has to risk offering again now that he's in a better place, and he has to let go that old thing in him of, "never be late to anything." (They are already an hour late.) He does, she does, and they not only make love, but they take back some huge ground in their marriage. All from a booby-trapped conversation in the upstairs bathroom.

Two are better than one,
because they have a good return for their work:
If one falls down, his friend can help him up. . . .
Though one may be overpowered,

two can defend themselves.
A cord of three strands is not quickly broken.

Fighting for one another when one of us is down has proven to be one of the most beautiful gifts Stasi and I have given to one another in our marriage. This can become as normal to a marriage as paying the bills and taking out the trash.

Heroic Love

The little matchbox of a house we lived in when we first got married had a problem with cockroaches. They would come out of nowhere every night. If you turned the kitchen light on, they would scurry under the stove or duck into the cupboards; if you forgot to turn the light on you would crunch a few under your bare feet. After about a year of halfhearted attempts to get rid of them, I [John] was finally fed up. It was time for a showdown. I bought bug bombs. I cleaned out behind the stove. I sprinkled powder in every cupboard. I finally dealt with those little buggers, and they left.

The Israelites had to fight to get to the Promised Land, and they had to fight to get in. Once there, they had to fight to clear it of enemies, and then fight to keep it so. David had to fight to secure his throne, and he too had to fight to keep it. God has long fought for the romance he desires with us, and he fights on even now. You need not be afraid of the fight. The battle can be won, and it will call forth wonderful things from you, things like courage and sacrifice, steadfastness and love.

What you need to fix a steely-eyed gaze upon is that part of you that wants to bury your head in the sand; to call the fight something other than what it is; to lower the drawbridge and surrender the castle. There is a traitor within each of us and *it* is the greatest threat to your marriage. The enemy wins, and you never even struck a blow.

You can divide couples into two categories and having done so predict their future with some certainty: those couples who enjoy sex and those who don't; those couples who are dealing with their brokenness and those who are ignoring it. But the most telling division is this: those couples who understand we are at war and are allied against the enemy and those who refuse, for whatever reason, to face the fact.

I'll put my money on the warriors every time.

Why do certain subjects always result in arguments for the two of you? Why is it that when you bring up the topic of money or sex, his mother, her mother, your brother, how much time you spend at work, your weight, where you will spend the holidays—it all blows up in your face? It feels booby-trapped. Yes, exactly. It is. You have just stumbled into the enemy's camp; you have just uncovered where he is working.

Now—what will you do?

There comes a time where you must turn and face it. "Okay, this is real. We live in a love story set in a great war. The enemy is having a field day with me, my thoughts, my emotions, or the enemy is having a field day with our marriage. It is coming after our kids. It is wrecking family vacations or our friendships or relationships. We are going to deal with it."

And dealing with it means you pray directly against it. You pray against it. This would probably be a pretty good barometer: If you don't do this, oh, once a week, you are probably being naïve. Satan and his minions don't take days off; they have no holidays. Actually it will prove to be one of the most encouraging things for your prayer life because spiritual attack responds to prayer more quickly than just about anything else. Not super easy, not every time, but more noticeably than anything else. You will both be so encouraged.

How do you learn to do this? If you are just starting out, we recommend you pray together the "Daily Prayer" we have included in the appendix of this book (see page 213). Thirty days of that and you will be amazed how much fog clears. We also recommend that you both read *Victory over the Darkness* and *The Bondage Breaker* by Neil Anderson. Listen to a series called "The Four Streams" available through our ministry, Ransomed Heart, at ransomedheart.com. These will get you going!

We live in a love story, set in a great and terrible war. If we will confront our battles for what they really are, against our *true* enemy, we can find our way back to the Love Story. It may take time, and repeated bouts. Of course the war itself on earth will not cease until the White Rider returns. Meanwhile, our hearts are created for heroic love, and you will never feel more alive than when you are loving heroically.

SEVEN

A Shared Adventure

God created human beings, he created them godlike, reflecting God's nature. He created them male and female. God blessed them: "Prosper! Reproduce! Fill earth! Take charge! Be responsible for fish in the sea and birds in the air, for every living thing that moves on the face of the earth."

—GENESIS 1:27–28, *The Message*

Suddenly it is New Year's Eve. How did that happen? Where *do* the days go?

It has become an informal tradition of ours around the turning of the year to do a little dreaming, allow desire to bubble up from our hearts. We take up pen and paper and write down—in a completely unedited fashion—all the things we would love to do in the coming year. (Part of this is fueled by cabin fever; it has been cold in Colorado and we've been trapped inside for the past ten weeks. Island vacations are calling.) It's good for the heart to do some dreaming; it pulls you out of the rut, and lifts your eyes to the horizon. Hope follows, like children running to the song of the ice cream truck. Desire awakens hope, and hope is *really* good for the soul.

We do the exercise first alone, then we come together to talk about our dreams and desires and to see what we might make happen. Here is our first pass:

Stasi	*John*
Travel to Italy	Fly fishing
A month at the ranch	Travel to Alaska
Horseback riding	Mountain climbing
Climb a "Fourteener"	Horseback riding
Visit friends in California	The Tropics

Now, we don't know what the coming year holds. But we have found that if we don't dream about our lives then we are simply swept along by the torrent of demands, feeling like hostages rather than mature adults taking charge of our lives. It is the simple reality of calendars. You only have so many free days. If you don't grab those days and hold them for all they are worth, they will vanish so fast it'll give you whiplash.

So this is a really good question for a marriage: What are you looking forward to, *together*?

We Are Created for Mission and Adventure

Every great story has its battles, and every great story is filled with adventure. This is why we love fairy tales, romances, epics, histories, westerns, biographies—any story worth its telling. The Bible is absolutely rife with this sort of drama. We come to love the hero and heroine *because* they rise up to face all that the story requires of them. This is deep in the human race; the longing was given to us on the day of our Creation.

After God fashioned this dazzling earth, he gave it to us. Which is a bit like giving your fifteen-year-old the keys to a Maserati. But, he has his ways of doing things. When God gave us the earth, he also gave us all of the adventures that lay ahead. No one had yet climbed a mountain, or sailed the sea. No one had yet written a song or a novel. No one had yet discovered that strawberries make wonderful jam. God has "hidden" joys innumerable in the earth he gave us, like Easter eggs waiting to be found in the tall grass. Someone will figure out you can milk that cow, and if you let the milk sit you can skim cream off the top, and someone else will discover that the cream goes wonderfully in coffee.

The earth is rigged for adventure, like a sailboat. And our hearts have adventure written deep within, like sailors hear the call of the sea.

A good story has adventure to it: an unknown terrain explored, a wilderness survived, a mountain won, a destination reached. And the *story* of how it all unfolded—or unraveled—is told over and over again. Sometimes risk is involved. Sometimes danger. Often deep beauty. Adventures can be had on our own or with a group. Adventures can entail discovering a new city or acquiring a new talent. The right kind of adventures help us to become more of who we long to be. And adventure helps to build companionship in a marriage.

Whether it is camping in the Tetons or traveling to New York to see a Broadway show, the excitement and mystery of adventure can be strong coffee for a marriage. The new sights and sounds, the need to pull together to erect a tent or hail a cab—and yes, all the tensions also—they awaken us from the dulling effect of the daily grind and make us more alive to our world, to each other, and to God.

Now, sometimes adventure is simply for adventure's sake, and that can be enlivening. But we think a marriage needs something more. It needs a mission. The highest of all adventures are those where we find ourselves partnering together for a *cause*.

Look again at the story—when God gave us the earth, he gave us a *mission*.

> *God blessed them:*
> *"Prosper! Reproduce! Fill earth! Take charge!*
> *Be responsible for fish in the sea and birds in the air,*
> *for every living thing that moves on the face of the earth."*
>
> (GENESIS 1:27, *The Message*)

109

Notice the mission is a *blessing,* as anyone longing for a sense of purpose knows—give me something to *do.* Something important. The meaning of the passage goes way beyond farming and fisheries management (though they are noble callings). The spirit of the mission is this—we are God's regents here on earth, sent here to bring his kingdom in all the many ways his kingdom needs to be brought. Oh, the thrill that comes when we begin to realize we have a role in this great story; that there is something we must accomplish with our lives.

Now, when people talk about their calling, it is nearly always as an individual. "I'm going into medicine," or, "I feel called to be a teacher." That is typically how we think of it. But notice that when God blessed mankind with a mission in chapter one of Genesis, he gave it to the man and woman *together:* "[A]nd let *them* rule . . . and God blessed *them* and said to *them* be fruitful. . . ." (Genesis 1:26, 27). "Them" would be plural, as in "the two of you"; "him" or "her" would have been the singular. God is making something clear: *You are in this together.*

He then illustrates the point in chapter two of Genesis. Adam has just finished his first assignment as governor (naming the animals) when God interrupts to pronounce, "It is not good for man to be alone; I will make him a helper. . . ." (Genesis 2:18). The fellow has just rolled up his sleeves when God calls a halt because something is missing; some*one* is missing. Enter Eve, Adam's companion. This is not about clean socks and pot roast on Fridays. God calls her Adam's *ezer knegdo,* a very powerful name indeed, only used of God in Scripture, when you need his help desperately. The woman is man's essential comrade; his lifesaver. And so the two are forever entwined—the couple and the mission; the mission and the couple.

The implications are pretty staggering—we have a mission we cannot fulfill without each other. We are in this together. That is God's gift to husband and wife.

Desperate Times

But Adam and Eve blew it; they failed to maintain a united front and ran the ship aground. They surrendered the entire beautiful kingdom to the evil one. Satan becomes "the prince of this earth" (John 14:30), not by original intent, but through treachery and deceit. The world now groans under his rule. Like every cruel despot that will come to serve him like a marionette, Satan goes on to ravage the earth and mankind. Then—this would be the cue for trumpets and banners—Jesus shows up. Not gentle Jesus "meek and mild" but a warrior king come to take back his father's kingdom, come to ransom us from darkness and strike a deathblow to the dark prince, pry this world from his wretched grasp.

What we call "Christianity" is an *invasion.*

The Kingdom of God is advancing into the kingdom of darkness, a campaign to ransom people *and* the earth God intended us to rule. For the Son of Man came to seek and save what was lost. *All* that was lost. If Christianity seems to you to be having rather less than a remarkable impact on the earth, it is because too many Christians have this idea that we are in a waiting game, that we are basically killing time until Jesus comes back and we all get to go to heaven. We are sitting around like people waiting to catch a flight. That is not what Jesus told us to do; he didn't say, "Now hold tight in those pews and twiddle your holy thumbs, I'll be back soon as I can." He said, "As the Father has sent me, I send you" (John 20:21).

Let that sink in for a moment. New orders have been given.

We still have all the joys of learning to sail the seas and write novels, and discover quantum physics. But now we have also been called up into the more urgent mission of the invasion. Jesus has handed us the playbook; he has commissioned us to carry on in his stead. Every one of us. Which is to say that our mission now is far more grave than it was when Eden was our home, and of far greater consequence. Isn't this at the heart of every fairy tale? The boy and girl find themselves thrown into an adventure and frankly way over their heads. The two of you are part of something beautiful and dangerous.

This is crucial to a Christian understanding of marriage.

What Are Your Lives About?

Most of us have not really thought of our marriage as having a mission, apart from raising children perhaps, or "making a good home." And the home is vital; the home is *home base,* the staging point for our forays into the world. Of course, you want your home to be filled with life and joy. May it ever be. And raising children, should God grant you the trial, is about as noble an undertaking as can be named. The "hand that rocks the cradle" rules the world and all that. Making a home and raising children can provide a rich sense of shared mission, provided that you are both throwing yourselves into the task.

But sooner than you think the children will be gone—hopefully off on their own missions—and the two of you will be staring at each other like owls wakened at noon, blinking, wondering, *What do we do now?* and *Who are you?* If "happy little home" was the extent of the mission, once the kids have flown the coop the sense of shared adventure evaporates. This is why empty nesters have a higher divorce rate. The children were veiling a chasm—the husband and wife were not really one. Now the kids are gone and they have nothing left in common. As one friend recently confessed, "I had no idea how much the busy-ness of the kids was giving us a sense of togetherness. The soccer games, the plays. But once they were gone, I thought to myself, *'Who is this woman?'*"

Besides, you do not want your children growing up believing that they are the center of the universe. The balancing act we parents attempt is convincing our children:

1. You are loved more than you can imagine.
2. The world does not revolve around you.

When your children are the mission of your marriage, it sends the wrong message—both to them and to your spouse. You want your children to witness the two of you caught up in the Larger Story, captured by greater things, so that they will learn to do the same.

This is a difficult mind-set to dislodge, this idea that the goal of marriage is a happy little home. Just look at the number of home improvement shows, the *size* of the many home improvement stores, the endless parade of make-your-home-dreamy catalogs. Most couples spend the best days of their lives trying to make their home a nicer place. It is not that this is bad, but the Christian couple has to reconcile it with Jesus' teaching on the kingdom:

> *Therefore I tell you, do not worry about your life, what you will eat or drink; or about your body, what you will wear. Is not life more important than food, and the body more important than clothes? Look at the birds of the air; they do not sow or reap or store away in barns, and yet your heavenly Father feeds them. Are you not much more valuable than they? Who of you by worrying can add a single hour to his life?*
>
> (MATTHEW 6:25–27)

> *And why do you worry about clothes? See how the lilies of the field grow. They do not labor or spin. Yet I tell you that not even Solomon in all his splendor was dressed like one of these. If that is how God clothes the grass of the field, which is here today and tomorrow is thrown into the fire, will he not much more clothe you, O you of little faith? So do not worry, saying, "What shall we eat?" or "What shall we drink?" or "What shall we wear?" For the pagans run after all these things, and your heavenly Father knows that you need them. But seek first his kingdom and his righteousness, and all these things will be given to you as well.*
>
> (MATTHEW 6:28–34)

Is not life more important than a new dishwasher? And why do you worry about matching towels? The pagans run after these things, sometimes trampling one another as anyone who has been to a day-after-Thanksgiving sales knows. We nearly lost our marriage through our gross misunderstanding of what the plot of life entails.

Love God, love each other, and everything will work out—meaning, we will have a happy little life together. Isn't this the dream of most young couples?

A beautiful you and a beautiful me in a beautiful place forever is *not* the right vision for a marriage. It backfires on you; it betrays you. For one thing, it ain't gonna happen. Not until heaven. You will feel hurt and you'll look for someone to blame if you hold on to this as your life's goal. And besides, the vision is too self-centered, too inwardly turned. Like a bad toenail.

It doesn't provide the sense of a shared mission God created us for.

If you have been married for more than a year or two, you have probably fallen into a routine by now. She gets up at 6 A.M.; he gets up at 6:45 A.M. She starts the coffee; he typically skips breakfast. Tuesday night you watch "your show"; Wednesday night you pay the bills; Friday night you rent a movie; Saturday you do chores; Sunday night you call your folks. This is human nature to seek a comfort level in life, a form of security through routine.

If you have been married more than twenty years, those routines are harder to break out of than the wagon ruts on the Oregon Trail.

You go to bed at the same time every night. You use the same shampoo and the same toothpaste you have used for years. You eat the same kind of bread and the same brand of spaghetti sauce. You get your socks from the same drawer you have been getting them from for thirty years. You drink your coffee in the same way you always have. You make love in the same way. And then you end up surprised by the agitation and irritation of cabin fever in your marriage.

Boredom is the death knell for a couple.

It is certainly the precursor to an affair, or an addiction. This little piggy went to market, this little piggy stayed home, this little piggy ate roast beef, and this little piggy went postal because this is exactly what the piggies have always done every day for the last forty-seven years.

So, what is the mission of your marriage? What are the two of you called to *together*? Can you name it? "We are in this together," is essential for the boy and girl in the fairy tale. Finding a shared mission as a couple is essential to a vibrant marriage. It might be the very thing to rescue a floundering couple, and it will surely take you both to a whole new level of companionship regardless of where you are now.

Our hearts are made to live a life that matters, a life of epic significance. Surviving the week so you can hit the food court at the mall on the weekend is not enough.

A Walk in the Woods

Soon after divorce came up at the breakfast table almost three years into our marriage, John made arrangements for us to go away for a few days to a beautiful lodge in Yosemite, where we had honeymooned. It was to be a time of rest, relaxation, and hopefully reconnection. Getting to the lodge was a harrowing journey—tense and dangerous, uncomfortable and long. Kind of how our years together were beginning to feel. But we made it to the valley and honestly, it was beyond beautiful. The snow was softly falling, the lodge was lit up by white Christmas lights, and the woods, mantled in white, surrounded the meadow like guardian angels. It looked and felt like some land right out of a fairy tale, or Eden, or maybe even heaven.

We woke the first day to sunshine and after breakfast got bundled up and went for a walk. We strolled in the woods through the snow and over stone bridges, occasionally stopping to take pictures. And as we walked, we talked.

"Where would you want to live if you could live anywhere?"

"What would you *love* to do with your life?"

"What would bring you real joy?"

We began to dream together. We talked about the centrality of the heart to the Gospel, and how we might bring the Gospel to the world in a fresh way. Though it was our relationship that was in trouble, we did not talk about our relationship. We talked about what great work we might undertake together. The Holy Spirit understood what we needed, and coaxed us along in our conversation. I became more and more excited as we spoke. We did not know it at the time, but God was stirring our hearts in the direction of a shared mission that would eventually become Ransomed Heart Ministries.

In the same way that God has hidden adventures and surprises in the earth he gave us, God has also written dreams and desires deep in our hearts. Finding those dreams and desires, and sharing them as a couple, is one of the most romantic things you will ever experience. A whole new world opens up before you.

As Frederick Buechner says, "The place where God calls us is the place where our deep joy and the world's deep hunger meet." How fabulous is that?

As John and I explored our dreams, it began to dawn on me that all my past experiences uniquely qualified me to partner in this project with this uniquely qualified man. My heart leapt inside of me when I realized that not only did we want the same things, but I was the right woman to come alongside John and help make them happen! I *wanted* to. Something deep in my soul was coming alive as we continued to envision what it was that God has placed in our hearts to do.

The doubts and questions about our marriage—that perhaps we had made a mistake—were being answered. Silenced.

A deep fear had crept into my heart; it was not that John was the wrong man for me, but that I was the wrong woman for him. As we walked and talked in the snowy woods a shift occurred. The revelation came that I *am* the right woman for this man. I realized that *God* had put us together; that I was particularly suited to him and that he was particularly suited to me. It was not by accident, mere chemistry, sexual attraction, or some bizarre alignment of the stars that we had been drawn together and gotten married.

It was planned in the heart of God.

We were made for each other. God had brought us together for a *reason;* the whole of who we were—our life experiences, our unique desires, our spiritual gifts, our talents, even the man and woman that we were on the road to becoming—all this fit together in a way that made sense.

We had a purpose; we shared a calling; we needed each other. Realizing this truth gave me a fresh commitment for our marriage. It gave me a vision for our life together; the future God was calling us into. Hope and purpose, clarity and desire, all rose in my heart as John and I recommitted ourselves to each other—to share in the adventure that God was inviting us into.

Twenty-two years have gone by, and both of us would point to that day as one of the turning points in our lives. It lifted us out of the quagmire of an aimless marriage—a naïve marriage—and called us up into the Larger Story. We began to seek first the Kingdom of God. Now, over the years we have lost that vision—and gotten lost ourselves as a result—then found our way out again as we recovered a shared vision. It has changed and matured, as we have changed and matured. And it has probably done more for our marriage than all of the vacations and dinners out put together.

Even more than the dryer we bought last week.

The Adventure Has Begun

"If there is anything more exciting than being alive," asks Buechner, "I'd like to know what it is." Our vote for runner-up would be marriage; at least, it knocks us off balance often enough to *feel* like we are on an adventure. What we go on to make of it depends on how we look at it. You see, the truth is we have already been hurled into a Great Story. It is happening all around us, all the time. The catching up we have to do is *learning to enter in.*

Step One involves a change in our perspective. We take the life we have right now, and we say to ourselves, *We are in this together.*

I [Stasi] had a really difficult conversation a few days ago with a young woman I care about. It was one of those talks I think we all avoid for as long as possible—usually too long. I had some things I needed to say, which I knew she would not want to hear. She matters so much to me, and I feared the conversation might blow up. So I asked John to be in prayer about it as we met. As soon as I got home John asked, "So, how did it go?" He sat down, his eyes intent on mine, waiting to hear the story. Coming home and having John invite me to share what had transpired was precious to me. We share in the adventure when we share in the cost and the triumph of each other's lives: "How did it go at work today?" "Have you made that difficult call to your mother?" "Tell me about your trip."

Remember the last scene in the movie *Jerry Maguire,* the "you had me at hello" scene? He comes back to his estranged wife to tell her, "On what was supposed to be the happiest night of my business life, it wasn't complete, wasn't nearly close to being in the same vicinity as complete, because I couldn't share it with you." Everything is better when it is shared. Caring about the lives we are each living is a way to share in the adventure. Caring enough to actually pray for one another really helps us feel like we are in this together.

I [John] still travel and speak quite a bit. Sometimes Stasi and I do this together, but more often I am alone. I will be across the country or the globe somewhere, having just checked into my hotel. I will open my suitcase, and there will be a card from Stasi. Suddenly we are connected again. Her words of encouragement, the Scriptures she often includes, and her assurance that she is praying for me pull us together in the mission. Even though she is not physically with me, we are one heart in the mission. We are in this together. She sends those cards with me every time.

We share in the adventure when we help our spouse not to lose heart.

Encouragement has got to be one of the greatest offerings of true companionship. You, better than anyone, know your mate's story, and you know where the enemy likes to stick it to them. You can see when they are down, and your words of encouragement can lift them up again. Like a bridge over troubled water. "Two are better than one . . . if one falls down, his friend can pick him up" (Ecclesiastes 4:10). Talk about your lives. Pray for one another. Encourage one another. Even though you may spend your nine-to-five day engaged in different places, this will help you feel like you are sharing life and not just sheets.

Step Two in finding a shared adventure is to cultivate an adventurous marriage. So, adventure together. Do a little dreaming, like we do around New Year's Eve. Where would you love to travel? What about taking up dancing, or an instrument, or learning a language together? Maybe you would like to move to a new neighborhood, a new city, or a new country! Just start dreaming a little as a couple. What are you looking forward to, *together*?

All the canoeing that we do, the travel, the swimming, the horses—it cultivates adventure in our marriage. We know it is not the biggest adventure God has for us, but it refreshes the heart (we were made for Eden—don't ever forget that) and it prepares us for bigger adventures to come. How you handle canceled flights, thunderstorms, and capsized canoes is a really good test of how you will handle the pressures of the Great Mission. You don't get to jump straight off the couch into the mission of your lives. Let casual adventures prepare the two of you for more critical adventures.

Now, the Larger Story is gaining momentum, and we have higher orders. And so Step Three is to begin to seek the mission that God has for you. Ask *him* what he has for you. Ask him to give you a vision, a shared passion. Ask him what the next step is that will take you on the journey.

"God, what do you have for us?" would be a wonderful prayer to begin praying together, and then keep your eyes and ears open for how God answers that prayer. Sometimes the adventure comes to us, as with a phone call after dinner that takes you to the side of a friend in need. For you know well enough by now that quite often adventure is something that finds us. As the children said in Narnia, "Let us take the adventure Aslan sends us." If you are even half-awake with a pluck of courage in your heart, you will soon find more adventure than you can handle. Which brings us to the other part of the prayer we should be praying.

"God, what are we involved in that we *shouldn't* be?" We must ask this as well, for we often find ourselves committed to things that God did *not* bring our way. People saddle us with their causes, family tends to assert its agenda, and soon we are buried in dramas that rob us of time and passion for the things God does have for us. Getting yourselves *out* of things you should not be involved in is crucial to finding the life God does have for you. Sometimes, he will use misery and unhappiness to get you to move.

Our friends Craig and Lori took an enormous risk and paid an enormous price leaving their home and family in Los Angeles to join us here in Colorado and work with our ministry, Ransomed Heart. The journey began when things got pretty sour at the church where Craig was serving. After repeated attempts to make things better, it became clear to both of them that he could no longer serve there. The painful disruption was part of God's way of preparing them to pay the cost to make the move into a much bigger adventure.

Test the waters. Some friends of ours are heading out next month for a two-week missions trip to Malaysia. David and Betsy are not career missionaries and they don't really see themselves becoming so. What they are doing is *exploring.* "We wanted to see what God might have for us together." So they signed up for the short-term missions trip at church as a way of dipping their toes in the water.

You might want to try something like that. Or teach a class together. Reach out to younger couples and have them over. The possibilities are endless.

Now, don't be surprised or dismayed that many of your dreams and desires are not shared by your spouse. Each person has a unique role to play in God's story. We all have a personal calling. This need not be a threat any more than other friends are a threat. In fact, some of the most beautiful expressions of companionship come when we simply lay down our lives in order to help with our spouse's calling. Offer to stuff envelopes, travel with them, feed the horses. Love is never out of season.

The Kingdom Hangs in the Balance

"We're in this together" is one of the strongest cords that binds two hearts together.

This is as true for the man and woman who know they have a great task to accomplish as it is for two climbers roped together on the razor's edge of some Himalayan ridge, or two soldiers in a foxhole. To share a passion, a concern, a cause binds two hearts together quite unlike anything else.

"We're in this together" lifts your marriage to a higher level than merely playing house.

For one thing, it will rescue you from making mountains out of molehills. You don't complain about the dirty dishes in the sink when you are plunging through a storm on the high seas. Okay, so he used the rest of the toilet paper and didn't replace the roll. This stuff is small potatoes when the two of you are fighting to rescue women from the sex trade or young children from slavery. Having something to fight for puts everything else in perspective.

Certainly you have met the kind of people that overdramatize everything—who hold grudges for petty offenses, who get entirely caught up in all the little socio-dramas of the PTA, the office, or the church. "Get a life" is what we often want to say, and it is the perfect thing *to* say—that is exactly what they need. They need a life so that they get their noses out of yours. We are created for adventure and it seems if we cannot find one we start blowing things out of proportion so that it at least feels like we have one.

"We're in this together" has helped us to press through many hard seasons in our marriage.

Sometimes when the relationship is the source of your sorrow, it can be hard to find it in yourself to fight for the marriage—but you hang in there and love anyway because you know that other vital things are at stake. You can't preach the Gospel with any sort of power while your home is a farce. You can't look for the favor of God on your life's great work while you are letting your marriage become a travesty.

We are not suggesting that a ministry or a mission can ever take the place of love in a marriage—not any more than children can fill in for true oneness between a husband and wife. But knowing that the dissolution of your marriage will have staggering repercussions helps to rally an inner resolve during those seasons when the marriage lacks the passion in itself.

Which brings us back to the Story we are living in.

"What if this present were the world's last night?" asked John Donne. How would you live differently? We love the question, because it shakes us out of our small stories. And truth be told, we don't know when the world's last night will come. But we do know this—night seems to be falling. These are dark times on the earth. The little comforts people have built their lives upon provide a thin veneer to the utter fragility of the whole fabric of human existence. Watch a little of the evening news; it doesn't take much to realize that wickedness is rising like a tide. And we have been given orders by our Captain—"as the Father sent me."

Last night after dinner a dear friend called. "Hating to bother us," she was wondering if we might have some time to pray for her.

Seems she had been warding off dark thoughts about ending her life, and felt she was losing ground in the struggle. Like trying to climb a steep muddy hill in the rain. It is exhausting; after a while you begin to lose the strength to give it one more try.

Stasi and I gladly dropped our plans for a quiet evening at home and drove across town to be with her. The darkness around this dear young woman was palpable. This would not be your simple "Jesus bless us" prayer. This was going to require sword and shield and an unyielding intentionality. I gave a quick glance at Stasi; it was such a source of strength to have her there. I would not have wanted to take this on alone.

We prayed, we listened to our friend, we prayed some more. Something broke and the darkness fled; the air cleared a good deal, and this beautiful young woman had a much brighter countenance. This would not be the last round, but it was the next round and a very important moment in the battle for her freedom. She would not take her life.

As we got in our car and pulled away, I felt this triumphant *YES!* It is a wonderful feeling that seems to come from deep in the bones—that heightened awareness of being truly alive, when something has called you out and you have risen to the call. I have had this feeling when fighting brush fires to protect a neighbor's home; and last year in the mountains when storms swept down and we needed to do an emergency evacuation off a peak we were climbing.

There was a time on vacation in Wyoming when our family witnessed an accident; Stasi and I were first to the wreckage and pulled a bleeding boy out of a totaled RV. In these moments you feel so utterly present; all pistons are firing and all senses are on alert. Something vital has been required and something in us rose to the occasion.

Our friend gave us a gift last night. It was a reminder, really. Stasi and I shared again that wonderful moment of, *This is what life's about.* We rescued a dear soul, we pushed back the darkness, we advanced the Kingdom of God. Prior to the call, Stasi was folding underwear and I was doing a Sudoku puzzle. Our dear friend didn't know it but she was about to bestow on us—better than any Christmas present— a renewed conviction that *we are in this together!*

Marriage needs this experience on a regular basis, as much as marriage needs sexual intimacy. It is one of the essentials. Repainting the living room isn't quite going to do it. God brought the two of you together for great reasons. You need each other, and the world needs the two of you. Together.

Two really are stronger than one.

EIGHT

Back-to-Back with Swords Drawn

One can put a thousand to flight, but two can put ten thousand to flight.

——DEUTERONOMY 32:30

We have covered a lot of ground so far in this book, and we should pause for a moment, and review. Catch our breath. Climb back up to the top of the hill and have a look around. You can get lost down there in the forest, even though the trees are really beautiful. Let us get our bearings:

- You and your spouse live in a love story that is set in the midst of a very real war.
- God gave us marriage, both as a picture of his love to the world, and because we are going to need each other. We are not playing house—we are living in an epic love story.
- Your marriage is a perfect storm because your brokenness and sin collide in devastating precision with your spouse's. Yet God is in that, because he is using your marriage to transform you.
- When it comes to love and happiness, we are broken cups. We will put untold amounts of pressure on our marriage until we realize that God is the waterfall; he is the love we are looking

for. The greatest gift you can give your spouse (and everyone else in your life) is to have a real relationship with God.

- If you have to choose between Companionship or Eros, go with Companionship. It is the bedrock of a marriage.
- You have an enemy, and it is not your spouse. The sooner you come to terms with the fact, the better.
- God has rigged the world for adventure. You have a mission, your spouse has a mission, and your *marriage* has a mission.

We are sobered simply writing this little review. Knowing as we do something of the *reality* of these truths, just saying them again has the same effect as what you feel when a smoke alarm goes off in your house, or the police call to say, "We have your son," or when you push off in a canoe down an unknown river.

And now you understand why God gave us prayer. If all this does not drive you to prayer, we don't know what will.

Why Is It So Hard?

A few months ago we asked four couples, whose opinions we deeply respect, over for an evening to get their thoughts and reactions to some of the issues we are addressing in this book. We did our own little Gallup poll of fairly healthy marriages. We asked them about prayer—how and when they pray together as a couple. They looked sheepish. No one responded. They looked guilty, like the dog does when he comes back from a neighborhood romp. I [John] was surprised; these are strong marriages, people who understand the nature of the world in which we live. It confirmed a fear I had—people don't pray much. Rather, *couples* don't pray much *together*. And why is that?

(Yet again, this might come as an encouragement—*it's not just you.*)

For one thing, you have an enemy. He does not want the two of you building a united front, certainly not in prayer of all things. It is far too threatening. I mean, prayer works and he knows it. So, he will do what he can to prevent it. You set aside a time to pray, and suddenly—the phone rings, the cat hacks up a hair ball on your bed, the kids burst into a fight or the two of you do.

Back in the tenth year of our marriage, after we had walked to the brink of divorce that second time, Stasi and I decided it was time to take prayer seriously. We went upstairs, closed our bedroom door, and began to pray, really pray. We heard a thud, then a scream; downstairs Blaine had broken his arm.

Good grief—how blatant does it get?

More often what happens when you try to pray together is that suddenly you feel irritated at one another, for no apparent reason or for every possible reason. Reasons you forgot all about suddenly return in a parade. Or you are at a loss for words. You feel stupid. You wonder if it is even going to work. Suddenly you are hungry; you start thinking about dinner. Or you remember you forgot to take the clothes out of the washer and put them in the dryer, and if you don't do it now you won't have that top to wear tomorrow. Isn't all this just a little too obvious?

Now that you realize the source of the distraction—Satan, your enemy, or one of his deputies—you are better prepared to recognize it, and push through it.

But there are other reasons why couples find it hard to make prayer together happen in any sort of consistent way.

Prayer is such an intimate act, a place of vulnerability. It is, hopefully, when we are our least guarded, our most honest selves. And this is good, of course; this is as it ought to be. When we come to God, we certainly want to come as honestly and openly as we can; we want to be our truest selves before him. Prayer lets us be in a place of need.

Now when we are alone, this vulnerability can feel quite relieving; it feels good to drop our guard. But when we come *together* to pray, yikes. Most couples are not nearly so vulnerable with each other. We have our guard up most of the time. We might not have known it, but we sure feel it when we take up praying together. It feels awkward and vulnerable and that is very, *very* good. If we can drop our guard here, the two of us looking at God, then we just might get to the place where we can drop our guard when we are looking at each other.

Praying together is an intimate encounter; it will cultivate intimacy and companionship in your marriage—*We are in this together.* "It's like sex," Stasi says. And this is why we don't recommend that singles pray intimately with a member of the opposite sex. Early in a dating relationship, it is not a good idea. It drops you suddenly into a deep level of intimacy; hot tubs do the same thing. I remember wanting to make love to Stasi after we had prayed.

Prayer brings us to a place of nakedness, and within marriage that is a beautiful thing. It might feel awkward, especially as you start out. Courage, friends; this is worth it.

Crawl, Walk, Run

Nobody is asking you to become Mother Teresa here. You are not being called up to become Benedictines. If all the two of you do is simply invite Jesus into your lives, into the moment and the issue at hand—whatever it is—that would be wonderful. Really.

"Here I am! I stand at the door and knock," Jesus said. "If anyone hears my voice and opens the door, I will come in. . . ." (Revelation 3:20). For heaven's sake, answer the door; let him in. We will be wrestling with a decision, or trying to sort through our finances, or worrying (again) about our sons, and one of us will just stop and pray, "Jesus, come into this. We invite you into this. We need your help, Lord. Show us the way." Right then, right there, in the moment. Simply pray, "Jesus, come and be the Lord of our marriage. The Lord of our home." This will do great good. Inviting God in changes everything. Maybe not immediately, not to your eyes anyway. But it is a really good beginning.

Jesus said, "The knowledge of the secrets of the kingdom of heaven has been given to you. . . ." (Matthew 13:11). One of those secrets is this—the entire spiritual realm works on authority. Just like all the kingdoms do in fairy tales (they get all their good ideas from the Gospel). Adam and Eve were given authority over the earth, to "rule and subdue." But they forfeited that authority and the devil became the usurping "prince of this world." Through his Cross Jesus cast the dark prince down, and after his Resurrection he said, "All authority in heaven and on earth has been given to me" (Matthew 28:18). Authority was given, lost, and recovered.

Now, for the purposes of the Great Invasion, in order to carry on in his stead, Jesus shares his authority with us: "I have given you authority . . . to overcome all the power of the evil one" (Luke 10:19). "I will give you the keys of the kingdom of heaven; whatever you bind on earth will be bound in heaven, and whatever you loose on earth will be loosed in heaven. . . . Again, I tell you that if two of you on earth agree about anything you ask for, it will be done for you by my Father in heaven (Matthew 16:19; 18:19). That is why we pray "in the name of Jesus, amen." It means, "by the *authority* of Jesus."

So when a husband and wife unite together in prayer, in the name of Jesus, it is powerful indeed. More powerful than Adam and Eve ruling before the Fall. "If two of you agree" is another one of those secrets of the kingdom, and this is even more effective when the two are husband and wife. The kingdom of darkness *trembles* when a husband and wife stand together in prayer.

And guys, I think it will really help us as men to engage in prayer when we see it not as something soft and feminine, but as *battle.* You have a warrior heart within you. It needs a place to express itself. A lot of guys shrink back from prayer because it feels "churchy" or something they are not spiritual enough for. But in your kingdom you are the man, and when you take a stand in prayer not only does the enemy cower but the warrior in you awakens. Get a few victories under your belt—you'll begin to love it.

We understand there are many marriages that feel more divided than they feel united right now. Your spouse might not be following Christ as you are; they may not be a believer at all. Do not despair. "For the unbelieving husband has been sanctified through his wife, and the unbelieving wife has been sanctified through her believing husband" (1 Corinthians 7:14). Your personal holiness and your walk with God have a powerful effect within your marriage. When it comes to prayer, you still have a great deal of authority.

Nevertheless, what you want to secure is a united front. Thinking back to the fairy tales, we want the king and queen to be as one when it comes to ruling the kingdom.

Listening Prayer

Making decisions is probably the number one source of stress, tension, anxiety, pouting, manipulation, and argument in a marriage. Isn't it true? Well, okay—there is money, and your family, and his parents. But you have to make *decisions* about money and family and parents, so I still argue that decision making is the mother of all marital strife. As soon as Stasi says, "Honey, we need to decide . . . ," anxiety leaps from within. *Aooogha, aooogha. All hands on deck.* We have just entered mine-filled waters.

So, we want to offer you what might be the single most helpful thing anyone has ever offered you when it comes to your marriage. Drumroll, please. Aren't you just waiting to hear what it is?

Learning to hear the voice of God, together.

Yes. It is the simplest, most helpful, least practiced treasure and it will literally *rescue* the two of you in countless ways.

The secret of the Christian life—and the Christian marriage—is that you don't have to figure it out. You don't have to figure life out, you don't have to figure each other out, you don't have to figure parenting out, or money or family. You have a counselor, you have a guide—you have God. What a relief that we don't have to figure it all out! We get to walk with God. That is the beauty of Christian

spirituality. This is not about mastering principles; it's about an actual relationship with an actual person who happens to be the wisest,
kindest, and, okay, wildest person you will ever know. If you know
the father of Einstein, ask his help on the science quiz, for heaven's
sake.

Think of all the decisions the two of you face in a month.

Think of all the *ramifications* of those decisions.

If you buy the washer, then you can't take the trip. If you can't
take the trip, then you'll miss out on some desperately needed family
time. Besides, the trip would get you out of the bind of having to
coach again this summer. But the washer is broken and what are you
going to do? If you change jobs, then your new insurance won't cover
the surgery your son needs. If you quit the job that is killing you to
look for another, then it could be months, maybe a year, before you
find another. If you tell your parents they can't come for Christmas,
then you will pay for a long time. But you are exhausted and you will
pay for a long time if they *do* come. All the decisions—it gets overwhelming. This has got to be the number one source of tension any
couple faces. You both have your opinions, your ways of approaching
life, and those are almost always at odds. It feels like a setup every
time you have to make a decision. Tick, tick, tick, boom.

Winter holds on to Colorado for close to seven months every
year. Seven months. The cold and snow start in the middle of October and hang on until the beginning of May. Like a Narnian winter, though, we get Christmas. So you can understand that we look
forward to spring break with a great deal of longing and desire. By
mid-March we usually try to run away to someplace warm for a
week, if we can pull it off. It doesn't really matter where—so long
as it's warm. Last year Stasi was giving a women's retreat at the beginning of spring break; I was ticked. *How did we let that happen?
Who was watching the calendar?!* We lost several precious days of

spring break. The closest and cheapest warm spot was Palm Springs, California. I began to scramble to pull it off.

Now, several ruined vacations have humbled me to the place where I now stop and ask God for guidance and counsel before I book a trip. This was a couple of months beforehand and I felt that God was saying, *Rent a house*. Rent a house?! Really? That sounded too much to me; there are plenty of good hotels there. I balked; he replied, *Rent a house*. So I get on the Internet and try to look up houses and it was overwhelming. There are a thousand and one houses on the Internet. Who can you really trust? And was that even God? I got overwhelmed and booked a hotel.

And it was a disaster.

Stasi was absolutely exhausted. She desperately needed rest, comfort, peace, and quiet. The hotel turned out to be a dive, the room as gross as a frat house basement, and it was spring break at a cheap hotel—as far from peace and quiet as Mardi Gras is from midnight Mass. It was a disaster. She was in tears, and I was feeling like an idiot. I went into the bathroom to pray. "God, you told me. You told me and I didn't listen. Forgive me. Redeem this. Show me what to do."

I got on the Internet and God rescued us. We ended up renting a house for the last few days of the trip, and it was exactly what we needed. Peace and quiet, sunshine and warmth, just what the doctor ordered. Because I finally listened to God.

We used to approach decision making like two countries negotiating an armistice. You know how this goes. First, you take a read to see where your spouse is at—maybe fly the idea by as a "casual suggestion," just to test what their reaction would be. "Nursing homes are *so expensive*. Did you hear that Don and Maggie just decided to have her mom move in with them?" Pretend it is not a big deal; hold your cards close, and watch their expression. Like a high-stakes poker game.

Other times, you know what you want and you simply demand it. "We did what *you* wanted last time." Which might be fair enough, but it doesn't make your will in this matter the *right* decision; it is just "your turn." If you are not in agreement, somebody has to yield, and more often than not that person ends up feeling a little resentful of the fact.

We often overlook the greatest help we could have, the third strand of the cord. Meaning, you have God. Good grief, take advantage of the fact.

Learning to Listen

It is not even Christmastime but I [Stasi] keep hearing songs on the radio that are singing about Immanuel, God with us. Today, I really listened. And I remembered. Oh. Yes. God is with us. With me. Right now. He was trying to get my attention in order to remind me of his constant presence in my life. He is here, right now. I can take a deep breath and lean into his love.

God *wants* an intimate relationship with us. He is not a God who is far away; he is the God who has made us his dwelling place. We are the temple of the Lord. When by faith, we confess that Jesus is Lord, he comes and makes his home *in us*. He could not be any closer. To talk to God, we don't have to shout. For the Creator of the Universe to hear us, we do not have to yell. Rather, to speak with him, we quiet ourselves. He is our breath. He is in every heartbeat. He tells us, *"Be still and know that I am God"* (Psalms 46:10).

In the same way, for us *to hear him,* we need to settle down, to quiet ourselves, and to *listen.* John wrote a wonderful book on learning to hear the voice of God so we will not cover here everything he said there. You'll want to read the book. Together. It's called *Walking with God.* We also like Dallas Willard's book *Hearing God,* and Leanne Payne's *Listening Prayer.* But let's review the basics.

God speaks to his people. It is normal. The Bible makes that abundantly clear. In the Gospel of John, Jesus describes himself as a good shepherd, and we his sheep:

The watchman opens the gate for him, and the sheep listen to his voice.
He calls his own sheep by name and leads them out. When he has
brought out all his own, he goes on ahead of them, and his sheep
follow him because they know his voice. . . . I have other sheep that are
not of this sheep pen. I must bring them also. They too will listen to
my voice, and there shall be one flock and one shepherd.

(JOHN 10:3, 4, 16)

How do the sheep follow their shepherd? Because they *hear his
voice.* Later, the risen Christ is speaking to the Church when he says
he is knocking at our door, and ". . . if anyone hears my voice and
opens the door, I will come in. . . ." (Revelation 3:20). Jesus said
that we hear his voice.

Then you have all those stories of God talking to his people in
the Bible. And all those stories down through Church history of
God talking to his people. Add to that the thousands of stories you
could gather right now, today, from one church, of how God has
been talking to his people. It's a real stretch to say he does not talk
to us anymore. Or that he doesn't talk to *you.* It takes the kind of
reasoning that leads folks to construct elaborate theories that the
lunar landing didn't really take place, or that the government is
holding aliens in Area 51.

Think of it this way—Eve is made in the image of God, right?
Then we should not be surprised that God loves to talk!

But most of us approach prayer like making a speech—we say
what we have to say, sort of rattle off the list of requests, and then
that's it. We walk away. Done. We don't even give him a chance to
reply. Can you imagine doing this to your spouse (well, actually,
many of you *do* do this to your spouse—and how does that turn
out, usually?). Prayer is meant to be a conversation; God *wants* to
speak to us. To live in an intimate, conversational relationship with
God is the *normal* Christian life.

It is so important that we learn to listen to what God is saying.

He never tires of speaking with us, to us. He wants to. What a great gift that we get to walk with Christ every moment of our lives; talk with him, ask for his guidance, listen to his love.

Learning to ask God for his counsel, learning to listen for his voice, has absolutely revolutionized our lives. It has lifted untold amounts of pressure and brought unhoped for amounts of joy. We could tell you hundreds of stories like the one about the house in Palm Springs. Maybe a thousand by now. My goodness, this ought to be essential for every premarital counseling program offered. But we've never heard of one that teaches couples how to listen to God as the *primary* way of making decisions.

It's like setting out on your first expedition to Antarctica. Even though you have never been there and your uncle has been there dozens of times, you don't call him to ask for his advice. You wait until you are stranded on an ice floe, at which point it may be hard to reach him.

Bringing God In

Last night, about 10 P.M., Blaine walked into the living room where Stasi and I were talking. He announces that he and some buddies want to go snowboarding tomorrow. "We're leaving at 6 A.M. Can I drive? Is that okay with you?" Stasi and I both know the best way to handle this. "Give us a second, Tiger." He knows we mean, "*Leave us* for a few moments so we can sort this out." You don't want the added pressure of him standing there, watching the two of you play "UN Negotiations." Quite often what happens is your child will try to play one parent off the other. "Mom said it was okay last time." Buy yourself some breathing room, even it is only for three minutes.

Then, we use that time to check in with Jesus, both of us, personally. Internally, we are asking, *Lord? What do you think? Is this okay? Are they safe?* We just get quiet, and ask the Lord what he is saying. Sometimes we have an "impression," a "sense" of what God is speaking. Sometimes we'll hear his voice internally (for that is where Christ dwells now—in our hearts). Sometimes, we will have a "bad feeling" about a decision. That might be God, but it might just be our fears, too. So what we find we have to do is surrender all our thoughts, fears, and desires to Jesus. We yield to his guidance. It even helps to pray that: *Jesus, I give you all my thoughts about this, my fears. I trust you. What are you saying?*

Because we have been practicing this for several years—and it does take some practice—it's not uncommon for us to discern what God is saying in the moment. I turn to Stasi with my eyebrows raised, meaning, "What did you hear?" I want to respect her in the decision. She says, "I think it's okay." "I do, too." The beauty of this simple act it that it avoids so much unnecessary wrangling, negotiating, and gallons of emotional energy.

Now, what if we hear different things? That happens, too. "I heard 'Yes.'" "Well I heard, 'No.'" The first thing we do is stop and ask again. "Lord, we're not sure what you are saying. Make it clear to us. We bind away all confusion, and we silence every other voice." (For there are other voices, as you well know. Sometimes it helps to order them to be silent.) Then, we listen again. About half the time one of us comes around to agreement. "Okay, now I'm hearing yes. I think I was just letting my own fears get in the way." But half the time we don't hear what the other is hearing.

To make sure you are following the math here, what I'm saying is that half the time when we stop to listen together, we come to agreement pretty quickly. Half the time we are not in agreement; and we have to sort out *why* we're not. We stop, and pray again. We also do an internal check to make sure we are really yielded to God. You have to surrender your agenda; otherwise, the act is a charade. *Sure, Hon, we can pray about this. But I'm not going to yield my position.* You will find it really hard to hear from God until you let go your rights and your agenda. Besides, you want to know what God thinks. For heaven's sake, he's a little bit smarter than you; he sees all the pieces you don't see.

We take a few more minutes to pray and get clarity. *Lord, what's up? What are you saying?* Of those stories, about half the time one of us ends up "realigning" when we push further into prayer, and we find an agreement. Which means that only 25 percent of all our attempts to walk with God together end up without a clear unity. That's pretty good. It's a heckuva lot better record than most couples reach when they just try to wrangle through decisions without God!

Okay, so what about that 25 percent? How do we handle that? The way we sort it through depends on the weight of the matter. If we're talking small potatoes, like "Can I drive tomorrow?," we just defer to wisdom. Or, if one of us has a strong opinion about it, we try to respect that and go with it. Heck, toss a coin. It is better than making a federal case out of it.

But on weightier matters, you want to give the process the respect it deserves. It might be weighty because there is a lot at stake: "Hon, I'm thinking about changing jobs." It might be weighty because one of you is deeply emotionally invested: "I'd really like to invite my parents for Thanksgiving. Are you okay with that?" What's so good about praying over stuff like this is that it centers you both back in Christ. Maybe you don't like her parents; it would be good for you to talk to Jesus about that. Maybe you are afraid of change, and you worry about money; it would be good for you to talk to Jesus about that.

If it's a matter that is really important to us, we will often say: "Let's sleep on it. Pray about it some more on our own, and talk about it in a day or two." Clear the air, take the pressure off. (You will find that quite often, once the pressure has been lifted, you do get a sense of what God is saying.)

God can get through to us by any means he chooses. Sometimes we hear his voice. Sometimes the answer comes days later, as we are reading Scripture. Sometimes it comes through the counsel of a friend or pastor. Sometimes he just changes our heart on a matter, and it's no longer an issue. Just keep your eyes and ears open to all the ways God is speaking to you.

You can practice listening prayer in matters of deep conflict, but we wouldn't recommend starting there. If you are new to hearing the voice of God, it's really hard to hear when there is a lot on the line and emotions are running high. But the point is, you can avoid a *lot* of conflict if both of you are willing to yield to God. This helps to protect your dignity, too, both of you, because you are not being asked to give way to his or her agenda; you are submitting to God.

Knee-jerk reactions sabotage communication. If it doesn't bring on a fight, it makes something in your spouse shut down. *I'm not bringing this up again.* Holding your ground on some picayune issue simply because your partner "won last time" isn't exactly helpful either. You look foolish, and it tends to make people dismiss you when you really do have something to say. You lose credibility. *There she goes again.* Letting emotion guide you is dangerous. Trying to figure things out on your own can be exasperating. Why in the world would you want to try this without God?

Yes, this can be a little awkward at first. But so was making love. Talking about old relationships. Saying "I'm sorry." Don't let the awkwardness be a reason to give it up.

It comes back to what story you think you are living in. If you are still operating from the "happiness view" of the world, you are going to cling to your agenda and negotiate, intimidate, manipulate, and otherwise make a fool of yourself while doing damage to your marriage. If you are living in the Larger Story of God, this dangerous tale of love and war, then you are going to turn to God as a matter of first choice, every time.

A Hundred Surprises

I [John] gave a talk on learning to hear the voice of God to a group of youth pastors. Afterward there was a book signing. I'm standing at my table—feeling a little bit like some guy selling Florida swampland—hoping that I don't stand here and no one comes up when a man finally approached the table. "I don't need a book signed," he says. I try to keep a smile like it's no big deal and I say, "That's okay," but he goes right on to say, "But I wanted to tell you a story." "I'd love to hear it." He looks right and left, sort of like *You're not gonna believe this.* "So, I'm sitting there listening to your talk, and not real sure what I think about the whole thing. Then you invite us to listen to God." I nod, eager to hear what happened for him, but also sort of dreading that nothing happened and he's here to tell me God doesn't speak to him. Too many dear souls have come to that conclusion because of a bad experience, or because no one has helped them *learn* to hear.

"Look, I'm not a mystic," he says.

I smile but I'm thinking, *Since when did hearing God's voice become something reserved for mystics?*

"But I decided to give it a try," he continues. "So, I quiet down and just sit there. After a minute or so I asked God, *What do you want to say to me?* And what I hear is this: *Take Janet to St. John.*" "Janet's my wife," he explains, and I think, *Well that's a relief.* "We've been wanting to take a trip together for a long time but we haven't been able to pull it off. Anyhow, that's what I hear—*Take Janet to St. John.*"

I'm thinking that's the end of the story, so I say, "Well, she's going to be delighted to hear that!"

He says, "No—the story's not over.

"After you end the talk everybody's getting up to go to lunch. I turn to the guy next to me—we didn't come together or anything— and tell him, 'God told me to take my wife to St. John.' "

The way he tells this part of the story is sort of in the spirit of, *Yeah right—Can you believe it? What am I supposed to do with that?* I simply listen.

"And this guy says to me, 'Well. I have been holding two tickets to St. John for a year, and God has told me they are not for me, that I'm to give them to someone else. So, there you go. I have your tickets.' "

Needless to say, Mr. I'm-Not-Much-of-a-Mystic became a believer in hearing the voice of God.

And you know what? This is actually pretty normal for the Christian life. Over the years we've heard a jigawillion stories like that. Ordinary folks, learning to listen for the voice of God and how he blesses them for doing so. God loves to speak, he loves to surprise us, and he has hundreds of adventures in store.

So—ask him.

NINE

The Little Foxes

*Catch for us the foxes, the little foxes that ruin the vineyards,
our vineyards that are in bloom.*

——SONG OF SONGS 2:15

I was walking up the path to our house this morning when I noticed a new pile of dirt in Stasi's rose garden. It is the seventh new pile in a week. Stopping to take a more careful look, it became clear to me that these rather large and impressive mounds are not (as I thought) the signs of some new planting she has undertaken. With spring here I ignored them at first, but today's pile is burying one of her rosebushes in a rather blatant way. The gophers are back.

Little demon-rats.

They hibernate like bears most of our snowy winter. Then in the spring they emerge with an appetite—tunneling, burrowing, and basically running amok in what once was Stasi's very lovely and treasured garden. The fresh excavations made me mad. And exasperated. I thought we had dealt with the little underminers last fall. I'm beginning to think gophers will join cockroaches as the only creatures to survive a nuclear fallout. No matter what we try, there seems to be no getting rid of these little garden menaces.

In the charming and romantic book of the Old Testament called Song of Songs, there appears a warning to the madly-in-love-and-somewhat-naïve newlyweds to beware the "little foxes" that ruin the vineyards. Now, we are guessing that you may not be a farmer, and so you might just miss the impact of the warning. We town folk picture foxes nowadays as rather cute, even cuddly. So the passage loses its punch. The metaphor was meant to invoke the image of "cunning little menaces you tend to ignore but could of themselves wreak havoc on a marriage." Think gophers in the garden. It works for us. With our apologies to Solomon . . .

Our Little Quirks

I ask you, how hard is it really to put an empty bowl of cereal into the dishwasher? Why rinse it and set in on the counter leaving it for someone else [read me, Stasi] to finish the process? There is a dirty clothes bin in our closet. Handily, it is marked on one side "whites," the other side "darks." John's clothes rarely make it into this bin; they are piled on the floor in our room. What's with that? I mean, what would it take—ten extra steps?

We are driving to my friends' house across town. John is behind the wheel and the road is as familiar to him as the back of his hand. Still, the words "You turn left here" jump out of my mouth with the speed of a gazelle and the thoughtfulness of an egg. John responds with a look that says *no kidding*. Why can't I just keep my mouth shut?! I pick at my cuticles. It drives John and the boys nuts. Absolutely crazy. My sons will now reach over and grab my hands to stop me when I'm frantically picking, completely oblivious to what I'm doing.

Some folks whistle. All day long. They don't even know they are doing it. Some people twirl their hair, or pick their nose, or can't seem to stop themselves from interrupting other people. Some have a favorite word that is sprinkled into every other sentence they speak. Some get strange looks on their faces, or make funny sounds, or laugh when they shouldn't. Some never pick up their socks, or put away the mail, or answer the phone. Some interpret everything that is said to them in a critical and self-deprecating way. Some do not pay any attention to what is being said to them at all.

Oh for grace. Oh for forgiveness. Oh for thinking the best of the other person.

Because we can really get on each other's nerves. And then what do we do? How do we handle each other's bizarreness?

Well, first, watch out for the warfare; it *loves* to jump on this stuff.

Remember that beautiful evening down in Santa Fe that John described, when we had dinner and Josh Groban was singing? We finished the evening off with amazing desserts and then the unexpected surprise that our friends had called ahead and taken care of the bill!

It was such a lovely evening.

Then I almost tanked the whole thing by not trusting John's ability to make sure the waiter received a good tip. John assured me it was covered, but I would not let it go. Tension rose; the enemy jumped in with feelings of accusation. We walked to the car in silence; the whole night could have been ruined.

We prayed, we bound the enemy, and John forgave my doubt in him. It pretty much all went away.

Remember God is after *your* transformation. Before you tell your spouse that they are driving you nuts, you need to ask yourself, *Why does this bug me so?* Does this get in the way of your way of making life work? Does it rub up against your style of relating? Is the issue really about your need to control, or make a good impression, or the fact that you do not like being pinned down? Okay, making you late—why is that such a big deal? Sure, you have to load the dishwasher—why does this grate on you so?

There is a good chance that there is a log in your own eye that you will want to deal with *before* you try to help them with their speck.

Then, when you are in a good place, you can bring it up.

Taboo Topics

There are just some things that are more difficult for me [Stasi] to talk about than others; sometimes it is just easier *not* to talk about them at all. Hurt feelings. Sex. Disappointments. In-laws. Money.

Spending. Bills. Every couple has their list of taboo topics. These are the "No-fly Zones," the subjects that one or both of us have declared off-limits to discussion. There are as many reasons for having them as there are topics we refuse to talk about.

What are your "taboo topics?" And *why* are they taboo?

Sometimes we post that "no-trespassing" sign out of mere stubbornness—a refusal to own up to our issues by refusing to let our mate talk about it. Sometimes we just don't see the issue as clearly as our spouse does (the forest for the trees thing). What is there to talk about? Most often the reason is fear—fear of exposure, fear of rejection, fear of being "found out." We all secretly fear that we are wearing the "emperor's new clothes" and somebody is going to shout out one day that we are buck-naked. We fear we are *not* all that we hope and pretend we are.

For years, one of the big taboo topics in our marriage was my family. As newlyweds, we would drive down to my mom's house about once a month and have dinner with her, and sometimes with my brother and sister and their families. Every time we left, John and I would get into an argument on the way home; usually before we got off my mom's street. She lived on a very short street. John would make some comment about what he saw as unhealthy family dynamics and I would come to their defense. Who was he to criticize my family?

But most times he was not really being critical, just commenting on something he saw, or asking me a question about how I seemed to be acting. But instantly I would become defensive. I felt he was making me choose between loving him and loving them, and it made me feel disloyal, bound to a lose-lose situation. What was he talking about anyway? He didn't understand my family.

It was a good ten years before I could begin to look objectively at my family dynamics and begin to ask my own questions. By then John had learned to be very careful before wading into those waters with me.

Another huge taboo topic in our marriage was my size. No pun

144

intended. When I was clearly gaining weight, John would some-times risk asking me the question, "How's it going with food?" I refused to talk about it. *No, John, you do not get to go there either.* I already knew I was failing him; it caused us both grief. Bound by shame, I refused to talk about my weight with him.

Often the one who wants to talk about the taboo topic is the one who is not so happy; who may feel the need to curb or enlighten the other regarding behavior. To bring up for dialogue an uncomfortable subject can be an act of immense courage. To *stay present* to your spouse while you bring up a difficult subject takes courage as well. And faith. Every one of us has little quirks we are entirely unaware of. Do you know what yours are? Want to risk asking your spouse? Or what about asking the question, "Are there things I do that really annoy you?"

Refusing to address issues in our marriage leads to hiding. And resentment. When you close off a section of your house, all the dark little creatures move in. You *do not* want to give the enemy this kind of playground.

Speculation

In my experience, it is *so* much easier for me to think the worst about everything:

> *John hasn't called because he's mad at me.*
> *My friend didn't drop by because she is upset with me.*
> *I wasn't invited to the party because they don't like me.*

Our thoughts flow downhill like water. If we are not aware of what we are thinking, our thoughts wander, leading us down windy ways through dark woods. We lose perspective; we start speculating; we come to terrible conclusions in about seven seconds. The Scripture urging us to "take every thought captive to Christ" is vital (2 Corinthians 10:5). What we think matters; our thoughts and imagination pave the way for our beliefs, and then our actions are soon to follow.

I know I'm not alone in giving way to speculation. But I want to mature in this area; to grow up. Don't you?

What I have learned (the hard way) is first of all not to judge *motives*. You don't really *know* another person's motives. You can speculate, but you don't know why he didn't call. You don't know why they forgot to invite you to the party. When we assume motives we usually assume bad motives, right? You are already mad before he walks in the door. You are already hurt before something is actually said. Yet nine times out of ten, there is not a real reason behind it. You jumped to conclusions. You speculated. He did not hang up on you, his cell battery died. They did not invite you because you told them you were going to be out of town.

It is hard, but I'm trying these days to assume the best. Assume their heart is good, and your heart is good.

This has gotten us through so many potential blowups, I can't even count them. Regarding socks and bowls, I can think, *John takes me for granted. He's thoughtless and just expects me to clean up after him* or I can think, *He was in a hurry. It has nothing to do with me. I love him.* John can interpret my giving him unnecessary directions as, *She thinks I'm an idiot,* or he can let it slide with a smile and think, *There she goes again. I love her.*

The other thing I'm learning to do is to talk about it, especially when I find my mind beginning to imagine the worst.

It is so much better if we ask, "Are you upset with me?" "Is there something it would be good to talk about?" "Are you feeling . . ." Just fill in the blank. The Valley of Speculation is the enemy's terrain and speculation does not lead to life. So many critical moments turn on *interpretation*. How many times a day does the great cloud of witnesses surrounding us hold their breath? *What will he do? How will she respond?*

You will find you also need to be aware of how your friends and family speculate. Not only is it easy for me to think the worst, it is easy for my friends to do so as well. They too will assume that if I had a funny look on my face when last we met, it must be because

I was upset with them (and not because of the migraine I was suffering).

If my husband is taking some time for male companionship or time alone to spend with God, I am glad for it. He comes home refreshed, more himself, and ready to dive back into what is going to be required of him. We both need time away from each other and away from the family. We need time spent alone with God or with friends. But too often when I mention to others that John is away, their response will be, "When is it *your* turn?" They are assuming that I don't get a turn; they are planting the suspicion in my mind that John gets a lot more time for himself than I do. It is a tit-for-tat mentality—an unhealthy and unloving tendency to keep score. This is so unhelpful. Questions like these can undermine the marriage. Love does not keep score.

Bad Timing

Timing is everything in the flying trapeze of marital communication. As Proverbs says, "How good is a timely word!" (Proverbs 15:3). This is yet another thing I have learned the hard way—with the brunt of the hardness falling on John's heart. He has borne the blows of my ill-timed words. I spoke too soon, and then it had the opposite effect from what I was after. This is not to say that I should not speak at all. But along with learning to carefully choose my words, I have learned to choose *when* to speak them.

John shares the story in *Walking with God* how he noticed he was coming home from work and having a little glass of wine or beer almost every night. Now, he was not getting drunk, far from it, but I did notice that what had been a once-a-month, once-a-week thing was becoming an almost everyday thing. I asked God if I was supposed to bring it up (I *wanted* to bring it up). God said, *No.* So, what I did was pray—I prayed for John and I prayed for God to talk to him about it.

The coolest thing is when you get to see your prayers work.

A few weeks later John came to me and said, "God's been talking to me about drinking and he's asked me to let it go. I need to give it up." And he did.

Sometimes it is not ours to talk with our spouse about it all; rather we let God do his sanctifying work, which he does so well. Sometimes we *are* supposed to speak to our beloved. Then we need to pray for God's help to pick the time and the words to speak. Choose wisely. Walk with God. May we suggest that you *pray first*! Ask God about it. *Lord, is now the best time to bring this up?* and even *How do I bring this up?* and even *Do I bring it up at all?*

She would have to tell him about that, of course, but perhaps not just yet. There was always a time for the breaking of difficult news, and one had to wait for one's moment. Men usually let their defenses down now and then, and the art of being a successful woman, and beating men at their own game was to wait your moment. . . . But you had to wait.

(ALEXANDER McCALL SMITH, *Morality for Beautiful Girls*)

Sometimes the line between loving wisely and manipulating is a shadowy one. But if our motive is to love, to aid, to offer, then that will help us to remain on the right side.

John and I find that if either of us is tired, or spent, it is not a good time to talk about anything. If we are weakened in any other way—emotionally, spiritually, having borne some trial, or another—it is not a good time. If we are in the company of friends or family and the subject could prove embarrassing to our spouse, then it is not a good time. Sometimes we will have to wait longer than we want. That is okay. It is worth the wait to ensure that your heart is in a loving posture and your spouse's heart is in a posture that is able to hear.

Of course, how your spouse ends up responding is not something you can control. But do remember you have an enemy; it is easy to get baited into bad timing.

Family "Viruses"

A friend of mine [John here] has a very cynical father. The man has got a beef with everything—the government, his boss, Republicans, phone companies, you name it. He would be great on talk radio. The man is *especially* cynical about women, starting with his ex-wife. "They'll suck you dry, Bill. Drain you for everything you got. They're vampires." Bill's wife began to notice that every time Bill got off the phone with his dad, he would become cynical himself. It's like he got infected with cynicism. For the next hour, or the next day or two, he'd caught the bug. You've all seen this happen, I'm sure. Especially within family systems.

Julie's sisters are men-haters. Julie is aware of it, and she does not want anything to do with it. She loves her marriage and she loves her husband. But after a day of Thanksgiving prep with "the girls" in the kitchen—talking, chopping vegetables, the camaraderie of it all—she finds herself "siding" with her sisters in subtle ways. Suddenly she notices all the bad qualities in her husband, whom she normally adores. She picked up something in the kitchen.

What is taking place here is more than just having your attitude affected by someone else's attitude (though that certainly happens—misery loves company, and all that). When Bill talks to his dad and Julie spends time with her sisters, they are stepping into the gravitational field of the family warfare. In Bill's case, it is the deep cynicism and bitterness that have pervaded his father's life. In Julie's, it is the mutual agreement that the women in the family "have to stick together" against men, who as a category have been dismissed. It is like stepping into a smoke-filled room. It gets on you and you come out smelling like an ashtray.

What is taking place in the spiritual realm is pretty creepy if we could see it. Those spirits of cynicism and bitterness are now trying to jump on Bill. If he's not aware of what's happening, he will let them. As he's listening to his dad go on about women, something inside Bill says, *He's right. They are a drain.* There is the agreement we warned about. He begins to make an agreement with the cynicism and—pow—it jumps on him like a bad cold. There are typically two issues going on here—you have the agreement, coming to you through someone else, and you have unhealthy spiritual bonds which allow warfare to transfer around family systems.

Actually, warfare loves to transfer any way it can, like spam. But add to this the dynamic that there are often unhealthy spiritual ties within family systems. For Bill to get out from under the cloud of cynicism, he needs to deal both with the unhealthy bonds and the spiritual attack. Scripture says that by the Cross of Christ, "the world has been crucified to me, and I to the world" (Galatians 6:14). You will find it very, *very* helpful to pray the Cross of Christ between you and family members—it keeps their warfare from jumping on you. Then you need to also break any agreements you have been making.

By the way, this is why it can feel so debilitating to go home for "family visits." You can't exactly say why, but after a day or two (or an hour or two!) you feel lousy, and find yourself falling into all the old family patterns. Often what has happened is that unhealthy spiritual bonds have been formed, or re-formed, and you have come under the family warfare. Heads up.

Now, when you see your spouse under this sort of malaise, this oppression, you have got to be careful how you bring it up. It is booby-trapped. The enemy will try to make it sound like you are accusing them, or their family.

Quite often after we'd visit Stasi's mother, Stasi would not be herself. I could tell she was under something—her countenance seemed distant, the light was not in her eyes, and she was moping around. "I'm overwhelmed," she would say, "the laundry, the bills, it's overwhelming." There were many years when this was Stasi's major battle. But it hadn't been true of her for some time previously.

And so, now my radar is up. I hear her saying her contribution to the family is "stupid" and unappreciated. And as she is describing this, I am remembering that her mother also felt overwhelmed and unappreciated, nearly all of the time. These were Stasi's mom's constant companions, her two biggest battles. These became Stasi's burdens as well. And so she came to the place where they became her identity—"I am overwhelmed. I am unappreciated." She embraced them; she made a deep agreement.

Now, the difficult part is knowing when to point this out (timing again). This takes love, wisdom, and a good bit of patience. You don't want to blunder in and trip the booby trap.

As Stasi is describing what's going on, I am aware that much of it, maybe *most* of it, is warfare. But when you are under it yourself, that is hard to see. It all *feels* so true. If I blurt out, "This is just warfare, hon," she can feel like I'm dismissing her feelings. Maybe even accusing her. (The enemy would love for her to feel accused; then she is further from getting free of this. I become the bad guy. He might even get her to embrace it more deeply just to spite me. It is an old ploy of his in every marriage.) If I go further to say, "You've got an unhealthy bond with your mom," the booby trap goes off. She feels like I'm accusing her, and that I don't like her mom. The walls go up; the conversation is over; the enemy has won. In that scenario, it could be months before we could even talk about this again.

So first, I want to let her know that I hear and I care. "Sweetheart, it sounds like you're under a whole lot. I hear you." This isn't "technique." I really mean it—I do care, and I do hear. Then, with love and kindness in my voice, I gently turn to the subject, "Hon, you know that overwhelmed and unappreciated were your mom's battles, right?" I wait for her to agree; it is important she sees it for herself. "Why don't we begin by praying off whatever of this is warfare, so that we can sort out the rest without the enemy making you feel worse."

What we needed to do was to bring the Cross of Christ between Stasi and her mother. It was important for Stasi to pray this for herself, to make the decision and assert her will for herself. Then she broke the agreements with "overwhelmed and unappreciated." The light came back into her eyes. The cloud lifted.

Family Boundaries

When our friends Jim and Sandy first got married, Jim's sister was in a crisis: Her husband announced he was having an affair. After a few months he walked out, leaving her pregnant with their first child. Jim and Sandy were renting a big house, and they invited his sister to come live with them. It was a very loving thing to do.

It was also the wrong thing to do.

For the next six months the newlyweds were constantly caught up in the socio-drama of the split. It was emotionally draining. Jim spent hours and hours counseling his sister. Sandy felt left out. Now it might seem like the Christian thing to do, helping a single mom and all, but inviting another woman—a very needy woman—into their home just as they were starting marriage was a bad call. Looking back, Jim realized he did not even ask God about it. Sandy got really hurt in the process; the whole mess was a source of pain between them for years. It would have been better to let his sister move back home with her parents; or, the family could have come together to help her get an apartment of her own.

The day God gave Adam and Eve to each other, he drew some family boundaries: "For this reason a man will leave his father and mother and be united to his wife, and they will become one flesh" (Genesis 2:24). The goal here is oneness between husband and wife. And the fact of the matter is, you can't "cleave" if you don't "leave." You can't become one unless you move family to a circle *outside* your marriage. When a husband and wife form a marriage, they form a new family, a new household; they are now the most intimate bond in their lives. All other bonds are secondary to this one and ought to *come* second to this one.

I was counseling a young man through some hard times with his wife. They had been married for eighteen years. "She talks to her mom every day. I just wish she'd talk to me." The deal was, his wife would get on the phone and chat with her mom for an hour every day. Now for her, this was normal. She had always been close to her mom, much closer than she had ever been with her dad. In many ways, they were best friends. It was comfortable to turn to her mom. She had been doing it for years. She didn't realize that the message she was sending to her husband was, "I don't trust you. I don't need you. I have somewhere else to turn." It was emasculating. She had never really "left" home (her childhood home) and as a result, husband and wife had never really become one.

You are a big girl, now, and a big boy. It is time to leave home. Let mom and dad, and sister and brother, go. You can't find true companionship with your spouse until you do.

The Pace of Life

We only have room for one last little fox, but that doesn't mean we have covered the farm. There are others; they breed like rabbits: money; disciplining the children; where you spend Thanksgiving; do you get a hard or soft mattress. You will want to ask God to reveal to you the foxes running rampant in your fields these days.

But one we have to mention is simply *the pace of life.*

Every age has a spirit to it, and the spirit of ours is frantic. Busyness. Run-until-you-drop-ness. Most families are going like rats on a wheel. It is madness.

Parents have the kids in every sport possible at every age possible, *and* music lessons *and* church groups, and good grief, where does it end? Busy-ness is soul-killing. It will certainly suck your marriage dry. There is no time, and no energy left for each other. In the busy-ness of life, we fall quickly into maintenance mode, survival mode, and getting-things-done mode. We take children to school, to the dentist, and to soccer practice. We pay bills, balance accounts, mow lawns, purchase groceries, wash clothes, and exercise our bodies.

It will swallow you whole. Do the two of you stop long enough to have a conversation? How often is that—is it daily, weekly, monthly? And how about doing things that foster companionship? How often do you play together, you and your spouse? (Do you notice how uncomfortable you are with the questions?) A frantic pace of life has got us all by the . . . throat. Without any ill intention, our hearts are separated from each other simply by the pace of life.

Now, are you open to having a conversation *about* the pace of your lives?

Does it mean less travel, less activity? What about the number of sports the kids are involved in, the music lessons—did you *ask* God about any of that? We feel swept along by the momentum of our lives, but the momentum was created by *decisions we made.* It would be very good to go back and reevaluate those decisions. How many nights is it healthy for one or both of you to be out of the house? How many weekends away?

Stasi's good friend and her husband, a pastor, take every Friday for their relationship. They are an extremely busy couple engaged in ministry together most days and most evenings. They need the time to reconnect as friends, companions, and lovers. They are intentional about it. That is their day.

Now I'll be honest, I have heard couples talk about saving every Friday night as their "date night," and I thought it was goofy. Something out of the book of "The Perfect Christian Couple." Cheesy. Now I see the log is in my eye; these folks are way ahead of me. I wasn't being nearly as intentional as I should have been with Stasi.

It's a slow fade when black and white have turned to gray.
Thoughts invade, choices are made, a price will be paid.

(CASTING CROWNS, *"Slow Fade"*)

Be careless about your marriage and it will soon show that you could not care less. There is an *intentionality* that is required. In order to find a shared adventure, in order to cultivate something beautiful between the two of you, you have to *choose* the pace of your lives. The world will not help you here; everyone is running around like the Mad Hatter. It will *feel* as though you have no choice; but you always have a choice. Always. You can choose to move toward your spouse with desire and intentionality. You can change the pace of things so that you can cultivate a beautiful life together. Really.

Generosity of Spirit

The little foxes are pernicious *because* they are little. Shouting is obvious; not talking to each other slips by. You don't even notice that you always drink the last of the milk and leave the empty jug on the counter, but your spouse has just about had it. Heads up to the little foxes.

When it comes to the transformation God is after, we are all somewhere on the road to redemption. Most of us are dragging our heels a bit, "creeping," like Shakespeare's schoolboy, "unwillingly to school." It can feel like your spouse has parked it on the side of the highway. And they may well have; you might need to talk about that. But even the best of us is far from the restoration we need, and we will drive each other nuts. Marriage is a submarine with Cinderella and Huck Finn shut inside. How do we keep from mutiny? From knifing one another?

Generosity of spirit.

It is the single most disarming quality a marriage could ask for.

Yes, there are some things that need to be talked about. You need not be afraid to bring them up—*after* you have asked God about it. But my goodness, if we stopped to "process our issues" every time our spouse does something we find irritating, we would never get past breakfast. (After you brush your teeth and spit in the sink, is it too much for you to rinse it out? Was that the last yogurt you just ate? You're humming again, sweetheart; I'd really appreciate it if you'd stop.) Most of this stuff you just let go. You simply let it go.

*A man's wisdom gives him patience; it is to his glory to
overlook an offense.*

(PROVERBS 19:11)

*Above all, love each other deeply, because love covers over
a multitude of sins.*

(1 PETER 4:8)

Remember, God gave you your spouse to help smooth *your*
rough edges. He is an immensely gracious person—and God intends to make you gracious as well.

Allowing room for your spouse to become who he or she is
meant to become requires giving them room to soar, or to blow it.
We must simply choose to let the other person's irritating nuances
or thoughtless actions go. Rise above it; forgive before they even
ask for forgiveness; keep no record of wrongs; wipe the slate clean
every day.

Love and war, dear friends, this is love and war. You are not playing house. Generosity of spirit will help you both so much. Then,
when there are bigger battles to face, you will not have worn thin
your love for one another.

TEN

When Storms Descend

In this world you will have trouble.

——JESUS

Mary became a Christian in college. At a campus Bible study she met Bill, a new believer as well. It did not take them long to fall madly in love. Devoted to each other and to following Christ, they were married as soon as they graduated. Upon returning home from their short but sweet honeymoon, the trouble began. Mary soon discovered that Bill had an addiction to pornography, which was vast and strong. As a boy of ten, he had "stumbled upon" (or been set up by the enemy to find) his father's stash of hard-core pornography under his father's bed. Bill was caught and bound at that early age and had been held captive ever since. (So often the root of an addiction lies in a person's generational lines—the sins of the fathers or mothers—being passed down.)

Every addiction wreaks havoc on the human heart and the hearts of those who love them. For Bill and Mary, his struggle caused division, sorrow, and untold grief. Unable to quit, Bill would try to deceive his wife by hiding his stash or lying about his life; it never really worked. For Mary's part, she felt betrayed, dishonored, hurt, and angry. Bill's addiction only seemed to worsen.

Over the years, Bill went to two different treatment centers. He participated in 12-Step programs, as did she. Hope would rise in their hearts for a little while. But only for a little while. The stronghold was fierce. Bill even came to Mary and offered her a divorce. She declined. But she was far from happy; she felt alone and in utter anguish in her marriage. Hundreds of times, thousands of times, her husband was continuing to choose a glossy make-believe woman over her.

These were going to prove to be very trying years—for both of them.

It does not always come as an addiction, or an outright betrayal. It does not always manifest as a crippling illness or a prodigal child. But however it comes, when heartbreak intrudes into a marriage, it can feel like our world is coming apart at the seams. The haven meant to be the sanctuary for two hearts can sometimes feel like the least safest place of all.

Navigating Storms

John and I were lying in bed holding each other before settling into sleep. Outside, the winter wind was *howling*. Our home is nestled at the base of the Rocky Mountains and gusts roaring up to 80 miles per hour were screaming around the house. The windows rattled in fear; I swear even our bed was shaking. The storm was whipping down the mountains, the wind hurling itself against everything in its path.

Sometimes our lives can feel like that; like the forces of nature and the circumstances of our worlds are hell-bent on knocking us to bits. Just when we think we cannot take one more thing to go wrong, something does go wrong and we tremble with the knowledge that the Big Bad Wolf just might be able to blow our house down.

Notice we did not title this chapter "*If* Storms Descend." Of course life is hard, sometimes unbearably so. As I listened to the wind assaulting our home, I was grateful that at this juncture in our marriage, John and I are unified, working with each other and not against. We are a team, united with each other and with Christ. And when that is true, we are strong and in my heart of hearts, I know that no matter what happens—and only God knows what will happen—we will make it through.

But that has not always been the case for us. We have seen some hard years. So have every couple we are close to. Navigating stormy seasons is a challenge every couple will face.

The limits of a book like this can be frustrating; we especially feel that here in this chapter. There is simply no way to address all the variables that play into why a marriage has hit rough waters, why romance has died, why a certain couple is headed for divorce, and how to find safe harbor. But let us offer some steps to help you walk through hard times.

The Reasons for Rough Waters

Two nights ago, Stasi was in an accident.

She was making a left-hand turn, hit a patch of ice, and slammed into a parked truck. The impact blew out the passenger window and pretty much destroyed the door of our car; thank God no one was hurt.

She called to ask me what to do. I am ashamed to admit how quickly I started jumping to conclusions. I wanted to blame her for going too fast; I wanted to chastise her for not using four-wheel drive. Good grief. My poor wife is standing out in the cold, shaken, asking me for help, and I'm leaping to accusation like a prosecuting attorney.

My only comfort—it is a sick sort of comfort I'll admit—is that I'm not alone in this. When crisis hits and something shakes us to our foundation, we all start grasping, clutching, and looking for someone to blame or some place to hold on. Like people do when they are drowning. Panic overcomes us; we rush to blame or to speculation or to a box of doughnuts.

Before you make another move, you need to ask yourself: *Why* is it hard right now?

Don't jump to conclusions. Don't start making unexamined

agreements. *We're going down. He doesn't love me. It's my fault. We should never have gotten married.* Slow down for a second. Your *interpretation* of what is going on will shape everything that follows—your emotions, your perspective, and your decisions. If you are mistaken, you will wander way off course and pay a great price. Take a deep breath. Put down the gun. Ask yourself, *Why* is it hard? What is this about?

I [John] remember the first time we went whitewater rafting as a family. It's a pretty exhilarating thing to do—careening down a raging river in a small inflatable raft, dodging rocks, plowing into standing waves, intentionally throwing yourselves into conditions that the *Boy Scout Manual* tells you always to avoid. Water was crashing over us constantly, and I'm thinking any moment now our little lifeboat is going to swamp (inflatable raft implies therefore *de*flatable, right?). "Do we need to start bailing?" I asked the guide, who seemed unaware or unconcerned about the volume of water pouring in. "This is a self-bailing raft. It'll flow right out," he said as we hit another wave. *Okay. This is normal. No need to panic. It's flowing right out. It's flowing right out.*

The hard and even scary times might be normal. Wouldn't that be a relief to know? *We are going to be okay.*

The hard and scary times might be signs of something more serious. Wouldn't you want to know that as well? *We need to deal with this.*

Catch yourself. Don't jump to conclusions. Walk with God. *Why* are things hard? Scripture gives us any number of reasons for rough waters; each of them requires a *different response.*

Transformation

Whatever else might be going on, you know God is using your marriage to forge your character. You also know by now that the log in your eye makes it hard to see anything clearly. So even if the primary cause for the crisis lies beyond you, it is best to start here.

For too many years of our marriage, I [Stasi] lived in a posture of fear. I thought that if John had a problem he wanted to talk about, it meant something terrible about me or about us. If we ignored it, maybe it would just go away, or better yet, magically fix itself. If I turned a blind eye to a tense situation or skirted around a painful subject, everything would be okay. You know, the "Queen of Denial" and all that. Just like I tried to fool myself to believe that food eaten in secret didn't count, I was an ostrich with my head in the sand hoping that problems in my marriage would go away if I just did not look at them too closely.

In his love God used trouble to get me to look at my fearful way of handling life, and the reasons beneath it, in order to set me free.

Whatever else their reason, whatever their cause, God will use the hard times to expose our sin. Our spouse's sin as well. It is best to begin by asking him, *Lord, what is being exposed here? What are you after?* Notice your reaction, your emotions, your inner thought life. Notice what you tend to do. Though other issues might be at play—are almost always at play—this is a good starting point. Accept your own transformation.

Warfare

You live in a world at war. Spiritual attack *must* be a category you think in, or you will misunderstand more than half of what happens in your marriage.

Think of it as gas on the fire. There may be a real issue between the two of you—unresolved anger, a hidden addiction, misunderstanding. That is the "fire." But it gets blown out of proportion, or it becomes irresolvable because the enemy has leapt on the issue prodding, provoking, and distorting. That is the "gasoline."

You'll find it surprisingly helpful to bind the enemy when things get hard or crises strike. The enemy may not be the cause of it, but you can sure bet he wants to take advantage of the situation. Kick you when you're down. Pray against the ways the enemy might be involved; bind him from your marriage. Get all of that off of you *so that* you can see clearly.

Ignore the presence of warfare, and you will find it very hard to see your way through.

Brokenness

A friend of ours has an eating disorder; she has had it since she was sixteen. Her husband—a devout Christian—has tried in vain to help her. "You've just got to be more disciplined, sweetheart." He made her write down everything she ate in a day. She continued to lose weight. He made her eat in front of him. She couldn't. He got angry. "You just need to obey God."

You would not ask someone with a broken arm to swim the English Channel.

So you can't demand the broken to live as if they were whole.

Discipline is not the issue; apply discipline and you'll make it worse. What is needed is healing. Sometimes the craziness in our marriage comes from deep brokenness in us or in our spouse. But we're so embarrassed by it we try to hide it as long as we can. So God uses troubles to flush us out of hiding.

What we need to ask him is: *Where is the brokenness, Lord? What is this all about?* And, just as important: *Where is healing to be found?*

Seasons

Marriage has its ebbs and flows; that is just the way it is.

As sober ol' Ecclesiastes says, there is simply a time for everything, "a time to weep and a time to laugh, a time to mourn and a time to dance" (Ecclesiastes 3:4). There will be times when you are close, and times when you could not feel farther apart. For no other reasons than that is just the way these things go. We don't really like winter much (so why in heaven's name do we live in Colorado?), but winter comes like it or not.

People have their ebbs and flows, too. If one of you is walking through a dark valley personally, of course it affects the marriage. But it is not *about* the marriage. This is really quite relieving.

However, if you can't allow for ebbs and flows, if your marriage must always be "happy," then you will turn what is simply a low season into something worse. You can whip a rain shower into a typhoon. If you can't allow room for your spouse to have ebbs and flows, take personal struggle, turn it on you, and then you really will have a mess. It's like picking a scab; keep your hands off and it will go away.

Check in with God—*Is this simply an "ebb," Lord, or are these signs of something else?*

The World

The law of entropy in a marriage works thusly: All things decline to a lowest common denominator. We fall to what is easiest. Stasi and I like to go out to eat. But I've noticed over the past couple years that we always choose restaurants close to our home over restaurants that are funner, or tastier, or might prove to be a new adventure. We could go across town or we could go down the street; when we are tired, we always end up down the street. After a while we are sick of the same old burrito, so we stay home.

The law of entropy happens in conversation, too; we fall into a kind of shorthand that requires the least amount of energy.

"How was your day?"
"Fine. Yours?"
"Tiring."
"Your mother called."
"Oh."
"Where are the boys?"
"At the game."

How many arguments happen for no other reason than that you are both tired? How many times is "sexual disinterest" not an issue of lost attraction, but simply exhaustion? The question is, *Why* are we so tired? Has the world crept in and stolen the life from us? Jesus, is there something about the way we live that needs to change?

Perseverance

There is a passage in the book of Hebrews we do not like very much.

"Although he was a son"—it is speaking about Jesus Christ—"he learned obedience from what he suffered" (Hebrews 5:8).

Dang. If *Jesus* needed to learn through suffering, well, it just does not leave any room for complaining, does it? How are we going to skip this class if he had to take it? Suffering will be a part of our education as God's children.

This is NOT to say that every bad thing that comes your way is God's discipline. It does not mean that marital crisis is some sort of retribution for past sins. That is bad theology and it has hurt a lot of people. A friend was suffering from a terrible flu; she said, "I sure hope I learn what God has for me in this, so I can get over it." I didn't want to be unkind, so I kept my mouth shut. But inside I thought, *You think God made you sick!? There are others things at work in this world. Germs, for instance.*

We live in a broken world; disease, accident, and injury are just part of life east of Eden. This world has foul spirits in it, too; they cause a lot of havoc. The sin of man is enough to sink any ship. Stir all these together and you have got plenty of reason for suffering. So don't go thinking that every bad thing that happens is God punishing you.

As Dallas Willard reminds us,

What we learn about God from Jesus should prove to us that suffering and "bad things" happening to us are not the Father's preferred way of dealing with us—sometimes necessary, perhaps, but never what he would, on the whole, prefer.

Not his *preferred means;* keep that in mind.

Though he brings grief, he will show compassion, so great is his unfailing love. For he does not willingly bring affliction or grief to any human being.

(LAMENTATIONS 3:32–33)

Having said that, we do have to accept the reality that suffering is a mighty powerful teacher. There is nothing that will get our attention like pain. The good news is, it has a surprising effect upon us:

Not only so, but we also glory in our sufferings, because we know that suffering produces perseverance; perseverance, character; and character, hope. And hope does not put us to shame, because God's love has been poured out into our hearts through the Holy Spirit, who has been given to us.

(ROMANS 5:3–5)

Hope is a fruit of proven character; proven character is forged through persevering during times of suffering. Some hard times are simply for our good. "Neurosis," said Carl Jung, "is always a substitute for legitimate suffering." There is legitimate suffering. There are certain things you never discover about God until you go through hard times; there are things you never discover about yourself, too.

And so it is good to ask God: *Father, is this from your hand? Is this simply something you are asking me to endure?*

Stand by Me

These are hard times for marriage. Family is distant for most folks these days. Community seems like a thing of the past; and church feels less and less relevant (whether it is true or not). We're all so busy we have practically no time for genuine relationships, especially together as a couple. And so we get isolated.

And that is dangerous.

No marriage can make it on its own. We need the loving support of others. For most of the past twenty-five years, Stasi and I have been a part of a small group, a home fellowship of some kind or other. What a relief to have friends who care, who pray, and who help us work through hard times. John Donne could just have easily substituted the word "marriage" for "man"—"no marriage is an island."

Don't make any big decisions alone—decisions to leave, to separate, or to end the marriage. Get counsel from friends who know your marriage, your pastor or priest, a Christian counselor, people who walk with God. You need the eyes of others on your marriage. You *need* other couples. In fact, it would be a beautiful thing to invite a few couples to join you to do the *Love & War* DVD series for small groups together. It would deepen existing friendships, and open the door to new ones as well! It would also provide a context for you and your spouse to explore these issues in a loving and supportive environment.

Love Is Insistent

One of the hardest days of my [John here] life turned out to be one of the most redemptive for our marriage. It took place during my graduate work in counseling. The program required that we undergo therapy ourselves. (This is a very good thing to insist upon; programs that do not require this border on malpractice.) Not only did we need to see one of the staff counselors weekly, we also sat in on "group" counseling, both to witness what group therapy might look like and to experience it ourselves.

The way the group worked was that we would each take a turn "telling our story." Then the professor in charge would ask the listeners, "Well, what did you hear?" Meaning, basically, "Pull back the mask; where is this person a mess?"

After I finished telling my story, and a few students asked some follow-up questions, the professor asked the question. Almost to a person, the feedback I heard was, "We don't trust you." *You don't trust me?*! I was hurt and angry. They pressed deeper. "You are hiding; I wouldn't trust you to be my counselor for a moment." I was stunned. What are they talking about?

I had become so completely accustomed to my way of life I had no real idea of its effect on others. What the group began to dismantle that day was my perfectionism, my guardedness, and my resolve never to need anyone. They didn't trust me because I didn't trust them. Or anyone, for that matter. It was a very painful experience. I was the "emperor without clothes." I was buck-naked all right. But it set me on a journey toward change, and there has been no greater recipient of the blessing of that change than Stasi. I'm sad to say I never heard her attempts to address my impact on her; so God brought me through that program as a sort of end-run to get to me.

You have got to own what *is* yours to own in the troubles of your marriage.

You have also got to insist that your spouse face theirs as well.

I [Stasi here] was really angry last year. It was loving for John to suggest I get some counseling. Now, he didn't need to insist; I wanted help. But if I *hadn't* wanted to go, it would have been right for him to insist that I do. The same holds true for John. For example, if he had not responded to God's prompting to let go the "little sip" of wine each night, then I would have had to move to the next level: "You need to deal with this."

For years I think we both thought that to overlook your spouse's issues was the most loving thing to do. I mean, geez, we are all a royal mess. We have got more than just one log in our own eye; most of the time it feels like a log cabin, like a tub of Lincoln Logs. Who am I to point out John's shortcomings? But then I read the verse again—we take the log out of our own eye *so that* we can help our spouse with the speck in theirs. By all means, we overlook their little quirks; we even overlook the ways they wound us, if by over-look we mean we forgive them. But this doesn't mean we turn a blind eye to issues that will eventually harm them, or the marriage, or the children. God doesn't.

It is not love to ignore your spouse's sin, or brokenness, or im-maturity. It is not love to let something wrong carry on. It is not right. Truth be told, it is a *lack of love* that lets it all go on for years. When you let your own fears keep you from bringing something up with your spouse, that is self-protection. Or indifference. God loves until what he loves is pure. As George MacDonald said,

Love loves unto purity. Love has ever in view the absolute loveliness of that which it beholds. Therefore all that is not beautiful in the beloved, all that comes between and is not of love's kind, must be destroyed. And our God is a consuming fire.

A friend of ours found herself in a dilemma. Her husband's tem-per was getting out of hand; angry and wounding words were be-coming more and more common. He would use foul language and call her ugly, horrible names. She asked him to see a counselor. He refused. So she moved out. She did not divorce him; she raised the stakes. It was a very difficult move. She had to support herself finan-cially; she was suddenly alone every night. Members of her church did not understand or approve. But it is not a loving thing to let your spouse carry on in damaging behavior. In anger he demanded she move home. "I will come home," she said, "when you go to counseling."

We wish the story had a happy ending.

He refused; he continued threats. She offered to go with him to counseling. He rejected that as well. Instead, he got his pastor to agree with him that it was his "right" as her husband to "demand she return home." (To be fair, I don't think the pastor knew the whole story; all he got was the husband's side.) Eventually this angry, unrepentant man filed for divorce.

You cannot force people to walk with God; you cannot force them to repent. All you can do is live with integrity, and *invite* them to do so as well. Take things a step at a time. Give them consequences when they refuse to deal with serious matters. And pray; pray like the dickens. Pray every step of the way. *Is now the time for me to bring this up, Lord? Give me the right words. How do I help them feel the consequences of their actions? What is the best timing?* Ask a friend to be praying with you.

Now, there are matters you are going to want to insist upon right away. Insist that the shouting stop. It is not "normal" for a husband and wife to yell at each other. Make no excuses whatsoever for physical harm of any kind—not to you or to the children. "But he says he is sorry every time." He may well be; but harm is being done and change is *not* taking place. Take the children and move to a safe place until he deals with his rage.

Is There Hope?

We feel a certain humility in coming to this chapter. We feel as though we ought to take off our shoes. Though we have seen hard times, and many, they pale in comparison to the trials that some of our dearest friends have had to walk through. And so we turned to them to ask, "What did you learn?"

David and Meg have been married for eight years; John performed their wedding. Last spring Meg's mental and emotional health began to deteriorate. Rapidly. "I was in a state of escalated anxiety and depression," she said. "We found our daily life fracturing under its violent weight." It is a dark vale to walk through, with many unsolved mysteries. What is needed? Counseling? Medication? Healing? Deliverance? They tried it all; Meg continued to decline. They found themselves "exhausted, bewildered, heartbroken." They went back east to lean on their parents, and to seek treatment.

When they returned to Colorado three months later, it was

on the thin hope that we might be able to rebuild our life together. We realize that in many ways, trying to "figure it out" is missing the point. The point is that loss is real. Loss is heartbreaking. And the question we must wrestle with is, when life comes crashing down, from where do we draw the strength to go on? How much restoration is available for a marriage?

It is a question many couples have asked—are asking even now. Last month David and Meg attended the wedding of a good friend. They heard the words "for better, for worse, for richer, for poorer, in sickness and in health, to love, honor and cherish all the days of our lives." Later Meg said:

We realized that at many moments this year it was literally our vows that kept us from jumping ship. Though our circumstances were unique, our experience of "sickness" and "worse" were part of what we had signed up for, recognized for centuries in these very vows. Slowly, I have come away from the cold breath of death and despair to hope anew that the reign of Love and Redemption is greater than the power of our folly and brokenness. That somehow, it seems, in the midst of broken pieces and shattered dreams, there is an active, loving, and generous Author who is relentless with an invitation to hope—that perhaps a life, a family, even memory can be truly restored.

Their choices to love and fight for one another and for the restoration of their marriage have left us speechless. Slowly, but ever so surely, Meg has gotten better.

Redemption

Remember Mary, whom we told you about at the beginning of this chapter? Although her marriage to Bill was hard and often a source of pain, Mary was committed to her God and to the promise she had made her man. She fought hard for her husband and her marriage. Mary *prayed*. She prayed hard and long, hitting her knees in the privacy of her bedroom beseeching the Lord through her tears. She sought the Lord and he answered her. After *sixteen years* of marital struggle and untold grief, God delivered her husband. The day came when Bill had the strength, the will, the desire, and the grace to say, "No more. I choose God and I choose you."

That was two years ago.

Mary is an amazing prayer warrior. Her heart is soft and her prayers powerful, often expressing themselves through her tears. She is a woman of deep compassion and mercy who *knows God*. She carries in her spirit such a sense of *his* Spirit that you just want to linger in her presence and drink from the well of what has been forged in her heart. The life she has with God has been hard won. The life she has now with her husband is a resurrected marriage—one filled with hope, forgiveness, and laughter.

Not every marriage takes *sixteen* years to turn around, and honestly, not every marriage can be saved. But I tell you Mary's story because as I sat with her, I knew I was in the presence of a truly godly woman. The holiness of her life, her utter surrender to her God, her First Love, and her "finally on the road to a deephealing" marriage were the fruits of a thousand different choices to lay down her life and love. And in every way, it was worth it. Whether her husband ever repented and was delivered or not, it was worth it.

Start Here

Jesus tells us about two houses and how they each held up when the storms hit:

> *Therefore everyone who hears these words of mine and puts them into practice is like a wise man who built his house on the rock. The rain came down, the streams rose, and the winds blew and beat against that house; yet it did not fall, because it had its foundation on the*

rock. But everyone who hears these words of mine and does not put them into practice is like a foolish man who built his house on sand. The rain came down, the streams rose, and the winds blew and beat against that house, and it fell with a great crash.

(MATTHEW 7:24–27)

The storms will come; that is a given. You need some place to stand; you need bedrock under your feet. When the winds blast and the waters rise—even if it's only *internally*—we have found immense help in returning to some very basic truths:

- I am loved. Deeply and truly loved.
  "I have loved you with an everlasting love."

(JEREMIAH 31:3)

If all the pain of the world were gathered together, and sorted by cause into great basins, the vast majority of tears would fill an ocean entitled "Unloved." Because love is the deepest longing of the human heart—however hard we might try to pretend otherwise. When things get painful in our marriage, the arrows that pierce our hearts carry some message of *You are not loved.* The arrows might be Rejection, or Anger, or Betrayal, or Blaming, or even Silence. But the message is the same: *You are no longer loved; you never really have been.* We have got to anchor our heart in the one sure Love. You are now, you always have been, and you will forever be loved. It might help to say that to yourself, every day. Maybe every hour. This is the boat that carries your heart right across that ocean of pain to the safe haven of God.

- I am secure. Utterly and completely secure.
  "No one will snatch [you] out of my hand . . . no one can snatch [you] out of my Father's hand."

(JOHN 10:28–29)

When we married, we all gave a part of ourselves over to our spouse; we became one, in very deep and almost mystical ways. This is why widows and widowers often feel as though, *I've lost a part of me.* So when things get hard in a marriage, when there is pain and distance and we are clearly no longer one, it can feel as though our very soul is on the line. You are in a safe place; you are in Christ.

- I am forgiven. Totally forgiven.
  "He forgave us all our sins."

(COLOSSIANS 2:13)

It is probably safe to assume—since you are reading this book—that you are the one who cares about your marriage. (If you didn't care, you would never have made it to Chapter Ten.) Okay then, it is also safe to assume that you are prone to taking all of the blame on yourself. You are probably the one who is going to be aware of all the ways you come up short in your marriage. What usually follows is that you start beating yourself up. Yes, you have to own your part in the mess. But you bring that to the foot of the Cross and you accept the forgiveness of Jesus Christ. Otherwise, your failures hang around your neck like great weights. All is forgiven. *You* are forgiven.

- God is with me. He will never, ever abandon me.
  "Never will I leave you; never will I forsake you."

(HEBREWS 13:4)

You have got to silence the power of fear *right now*. Fear, anxiety, uncertainty, panic—they won't lead to one good thing. Not one. Quite often the fear is the unknown future: *Will we make it? What is going to happen to me? What is going to happen to the kids?* You are secure. God will not abandon you. Emotionally, financially, and physically, you are going to be okay. Calm down.

173

When things get hard in a marriage, it can feel like the foundations of your life are giving way. It is good to remember that our foundation *is* firm, based on the finished work of Jesus Christ for us. There are some things that remain true, at all times and for all of God's children no matter what. It's good to let your mind and your heart rest in these truths. Read these aloud. Remember:

I am loved.
I am secure.
I am forgiven.
God is with me.

Type these up and keep them handy for when the storms come. Paste them in your journal. Tape them to the bathroom mirror.

For the storms will come, beloved. The wind will howl and the waters will rise. And Jesus, who calmed the storm, who is indeed able to calm all storms, is now and ever will be your help in times of trouble.

ELEVEN

The Chapter on Sex

Drink your fill, O lovers.

—SONG OF SONGS 5:1

When we started mapping out this book, we knew we wanted to speak to the issues entangled with sex. But now that we are here, we are having second thoughts. *Dear Lord—we're going to include a chapter on sex? What in heaven's name do we say? What stories do we tell?*

We decided to keep the whole chapter to three lines:

You need to do it. Often. In a way you both enjoy it. Immensely.
If this isn't the case, then you need to deal with why it isn't.
'Cause you need to do it. Often. In a way you both enjoy it. Immensely.

We were only partly joking, but why the need to make jokes? What are we all so nervous about? What is it about sex that makes it the most awkward thing to talk about—one of the classic "No-fly Zones"—even among couples who have been married for years? (Do you two talk about your sex life much? With ease?) Isn't it because it touches upon who we are, how we are doing *as* a man and a woman, and because the nakedness of sex is far more than physical?

Genesis says, "Now, although Adam and his wife were both naked, neither of them felt any shame" (Genesis 2:25). Wow. There is an abandon being described there, a freedom with their bodies, with each other's body, with their sexuality and their selves. What if we could get back to that?!

I was eavesdropping on a conversation between two couples—both empty nesters—about what it's like when the kids are gone:

"It's wonderful—we have more time for Bible study," one couple said.

Bible study?! Are you crazy?

"We get to walk around the house naked and make love whenever we want!" the other couple said.

One of those couples is far closer to Eden than the other, and it ain't the one with the concordance on the nightstand.

It comes as a surprise to folks unfamiliar with the Bible how much God talks about sex, and with such, shall we say, *enthusiasm.* The stern commands are only part of the picture, given not in the spirit of "It really would be best if you simply stayed away," but more like the final briefing before new recruits go skydiving. The commands are all protection; they come from an appreciation of how wild and powerful sex is, how dangerous these skies can be, and how glorious.

There are three things that are too amazing for me,
four that I do not understand:
the way of an eagle in the sky,
the way of a snake on a rock,
the way of a ship on the high seas,
and the way of a man with a maiden.

(PROVERBS 30:18–19)

Read the passage again. The author is trying to explore the mystery of sex, and using *poetry* to do it (which is probably the only way—no technical manuals here). Did you notice the connections? An eagle in the sky, high and lifted up, rising above the earth. Sex is transcendent. Sex helps us to rise above the petty, the little foxes. In fact for sex to be good, we *have to* transcend ourselves as we love one another. Which is one of its greatest gifts—to be free, if but for a moment, from that constant self-consciousness that besets mankind. Sex ought to lift you above yourself; it ought to be soaring.

A snake on a rock is usually warming itself, soaking in the rays of the sun and the heat radiating from the earth. The poem takes us from the transcendent to the earthy. It is hot and sweaty. Often Stasi and I draw close to one another and lie there warming ourselves to each other, warming to our bodies again, warming to the act. And when the snake begins to move, it is graceful and undulating.

Then the writer uses the metaphor of a ship on the high seas. Holy cow, these Bible guys really got it right—sex as a storm. Sex as a ship carried along by a tempest—waves crashing over the decks, all hands holding on for dear life. We are meant to be swept up into it, carried along by its power and majesty. There is no such thing as "safe" sex; this is not something you can control, nor do you really want to (though Lord knows in our fear and woundedness we do try to control it). The surging power of sex ought to humble us, unnerve us, cause us to want to learn its ways like sailors so that we can at least trim our sails, turn our bows into the oncoming waves, and make the most of the careening ride. To be foolish with sex is to risk violence and destruction (that is where the stern commands come in). But after the storm has passed, we feel a sense of awe, of worship even.

God has created the human form and the human heart to experience passion and ecstasy when we are fully loving one another—transcendent, earthy, tempestuous. It is a gift he intended us to enjoy. Often. This ought to change your view of God—he is intense about pleasure! At the center of the Song of Songs, as the two lovers are really going at it full throttle, God speaks, and what he says is this: "Drink your fill, O lovers" (Song of Songs 5:1). Drink your fill. Let's see if we can find our way back into that.

Wholehearted Sex

You can have sex outside of marriage, as any teenager knows.

You can experience orgasm and ecstasy outside marriage. For a time.

But marriage is the sanctuary God created for sex, and only there, in the refuge of covenantal love, will you find sex at its best. For a lifetime. The coming together of two bodies in the sensual fireworks of sex is meant to be a *consummating* act, the climactic event of two hearts and souls that have already been coming together outside the bedroom and can't wait to complete the intimacy as deeply as they possibly can. "I *want* you" says it all. The passion comes from the soul; the opening movements of this symphony take place well before there are four bare legs in bed.

So let us begin here: *Sex when there is love is the best sex of all.*

Giving sex without love borders on prostitution. Demanding sex without love is abuse. We are talking about the intertwining of two *hearts* as their bodies become one. The more you have that in mind the better things will go.

And so God gave us woman. She is aroused by *relationship,* by tender words, by acts of strength offered far outside the bedroom and far beforehand. (Thus the adage "sex begins in the kitchen," which most men misunderstand as "doing it" in the kitchen as well as the bedroom. Sorry fellas; the floor is cold anyway. This is about wooing her heart.) For a woman to give herself over to her husband fully—which is sex as it ought to be—he has to have won her heart, and won it again if only in small, simple ways today. If she is going to be able to abandon herself—which is almost always essential to her orgasm—her man is going to have to have paid attention to the *relationship.*

How beautiful of God to do that; it is so arresting. There are no shortcuts. This act is meant to be the climax of intimacy.

I have counseled many married women who have told me, "I'll give him my body. But not my soul." The reason being that "he" has not won the right to enter her soul, and I would argue he has therefore not won the right to enter her body. When a woman opens herself up for her man, it is an act of stunning vulnerability. This kind of inviting openness can only be won through love and trust. God thus builds into the sexual mystery an *insistence* upon love and trust outside of bed. How true to his character; it does not work to come to God for the "goodies"—answered prayers, blessings of whatever sort—apart from a relationship with him. The treasures are for those who love him, and *live* like it.

So it is with a woman.

While we are speaking of Eve, notice that God also creates her sexuality in such a way that she often—not always, but often—has a sexual crescendo that requires more time than her man's. He is a stick of dynamite; she is a geyser. He has a short fuse and then wow; she builds and builds and then hallelujah. Why would God do this? Why introduce more frustration into an already tenuous and awkward environment? The stark contrast in our arousal and orgasm must have some design to it.

This, too, is absolutely beautiful. There is no wham-bam-thank-you-ma'am allowed. What is God asking of a man when he creates Eve's sexuality in such a way that Adam can't just "do it"? There is a holding back for him—a wooing and loving and foreplay—so that *she* can be as fully enrapt as *he* wants to be.

How utterly lovely. It requires unselfishness on his part.

Now, let me [Stasi] turn the tables lest you think this is all selflessness for Adam. The scariest thing a woman ever offers is her beauty—right, ladies? And it is our beauty Adam yearns for. It is our beauty he needs in order to be interested. Now I am not merely talking about physical beauty, though that is part of it. The secret of Eve is that every woman holds (and hides) within her an inner beauty. Every woman. It is her feminine heart, and when offered with her feminine sexuality it is stunning. Most women doubt their beauty. Deeply. Though I have noticed that when photos are called for at some family event or party, a woman will "turn on" her beauty for the camera; she will "come forth," if only for a moment, so as to be seen as beautiful.

There is a choice involved.

The beauty of Adam's sexuality is that it requires Eve to come out of hiding, too. Men typically want sex more often than women (though none of these are hard and fast rules; we are speaking in general terms which have proven true down through history). Men want sex more often and they are more "ready" for it than women. What does this require of Eve? That we take risks; that we come out of our comfort zone. Most women hide in busy-ness and efficiency; every last one of us doubts we have a beauty to offer. And so for a woman to offer herself to her man requires love, and courage; it requires her to put him first, even as her sexuality asks him to put her first.

The sexual act is a stunning picture of what a man and woman essentially offer one another in every aspect of life. It is a metaphor, a passion play on what it means to be masculine and feminine.

Strength and Beauty

Permit us a delicate analogy. When they are making love, the man penetrates his woman as he offers his strength. The woman invites the man into herself. If the man will not rise to the occasion, there will be no intercourse, no fireworks. He must move; his strength must come forth before he can enter her. If he is passive, it will not happen. But neither will the love consummate unless the woman opens herself to him. If she is guarded, no union will take place. The man enters his woman and offers her his strength; she draws him in, embraces and envelops him. And that is how life is created.

Many things go into a good marriage, but at the core it is essentially *strength* and *beauty*. This goes way beyond sex. It is a reality that permeates every aspect of our lives as men and women.

A man bears the image of God in many ways, but most essentially in his strength. Not with big muscles, but with courage, engagement, and taking the initiative. Ladies, have you ever wondered what the whole superhero thing is all about? Or NASCAR? Fight clubs? Football? Army? Hockey? Why do guys love to watch shows like *Demolished in Sixty Seconds*? Why do football players do the little dance thing when they score a touchdown? A man wants to feel *powerful*. It is essential to his design.

Notice that the seductress in movies is often the "helpless" woman who makes the man *feel* like a man. "I think you are amazing," she says with a bat of her eyes and the signal that she is all his, and bam—he's hooked. She made him feel powerful.

A woman bears the image of God in many ways, too, but most essentially in her beauty. Not the perfect figure, but her tenderness, vulnerability, and allure. Guys, have you ever wondered what the whole romance thing is about? The *Sense and Sensibility/Bridges of Madison County*–type movies? Pedicures? Why gray roots cause her to rush to the salon? Why she loves weddings? Why she loves romance novels? Why she loves to watch the *Academy Awards*? A woman wants to be pursued; she wants to feel desirable, *beautiful*. It is essential to her design.

Notice that the gigolo in movies is always the man who wants to talk to her, wants to know her feelings, and to make her feel beautiful. "You are the most beautiful woman in the world," he says, "and I would do anything for you." Bam, she's hooked. He made her feel beautiful.

This all plays itself out in hundreds of ways before we ever jump between the sheets. A man offers strength when he simply engages her at the end of his day; he turns off ESPN, turns to his wife, and asks: "How are you? Tell me about your day." (These things don't always have to be dramatic.) A man engages when he protects his wife from a controlling mother: "She's not available right now. She'll call you in a couple of days." And when he provides a place for her emotions—without being consumed by them—and offers tender understanding.

A woman offers beauty when she offers kindness. The world does not provide tenderness or mercy on a regular basis and we all need it. Offering your husband a safe harbor for his thoughts, concerns, or doubts, and not giving way to fear yourself is a beautiful expression of your love. Seeing your husband's strength and telling him what you see feeds his soul. One of the most priceless gifts a woman can give her husband is the message that she *believes in him;* he is the real deal; he is a real *man.* We offer beauty when we do not fear his masculinity nor our femininity. Wearing a pretty nightgown is just one tangible picture of embracing both. For a woman to wear a piece of lingerie feels exceedingly risky. Exactly. It is vulnerable. Letting down your guard and offering your tender vulnerability to your husband conveys a message to him of beauty beyond words.

When a man goes passive, it is a compromise of his very essence. And it hurts the people around him. He can starve his wife by refusing to talk to her; he can make her feel utterly abandoned by refusing to engage in her life. That is why a man loves a woman by offering his strength.

When a woman goes hard, it is a compromise of her very essence. And it hurts the people around her. She can emasculate her man through her controlling efficiency and her refusal to be vulnerable. She can starve her husband through her busy-ness and unavailability. That is why a woman loves a man by offering her beauty.

Taking Risks

A friend of ours was getting married soon, and I [Stasi here] wanted to buy her something lovely for her honeymoon—something lacey and pretty and *small.* I went to the lingerie department of a local store and began to look at all the pretty things offered. So much to choose from! My eye was caught by a silky long pink number that reminded me of what I had worn on my wedding night. I went over to it and as I fingered it, I looked up and saw that I was in the "Misses" section of the store. Large sizes—1X, 2X, 3X. My sizes. I immediately thought, *Oh brother. This would look terrible on me.* But as soon as I thought it, I felt the invitation of the Holy Spirit to *try it on.* I felt shy and embarrassed but was moved by a deeper longing; so I grabbed the nightgown and headed for the dressing rooms. How long had it been since I had purchased something like this for me, for John? More than a decade.

I tried on the nightgown with superhuman speed. I gave myself a microsecond glance over and decided to buy it.

Now, it was two weeks later and my husband still had not seen it. John and I were going to travel to Boulder, Colorado, where he would perform the marriage ceremony between this young couple. Packing for the trip, the nightgown dared me from the drawer. I sensed God urging me to bring it, wear it, offer myself to John intentionally, vulnerably. So I carefully wrapped the negligee in tissue paper and hid it in my suitcase. I did not pack any backup nightgowns. I was committed.

After the rehearsal dinner, John and I returned to our hotel room. Going up the elevator, I was already nervous. Initiating intimacy is not something I do regularly or easily. The nightgown was a clear message that I was initiating. Yikes.

John brushed his teeth and then sat on the bed going over his notes, preparing for the next day. I went into the bathroom to get ready for bed and to change into the slinky number. How I regretted not bringing a backup nightie—my usual well-worn Hefty bag of a nightgown. I was stuck; I had to wear the new siren song. I brushed my teeth. I brushed my hair. I put it on. I prayed, *Help me God! Come into this! Give me courage! Please let this go well!*

I did not feel sexy or attractive in the least. I was majorly overweight and fighting a losing battle on that front. Accusations flew through my mind that I looked ridiculous, that I was ridiculous. But God was inviting me to come out from under the accusation that froze me and offer to my husband the beauty that *I did have.* I prayed some more. And then walked out the door and stood at the base of the bed.

John looked up, surprised, and said, "Oh! Pretty!"

Then he looked back down again and went back to his work.

Oh dear. This was not what was supposed to happen. What do I do now? I grabbed a hotel magazine and sat down on my side of the bed. I tried to lounge there seductively. I found that this nightgown wasn't meant for sitting in. It was uncomfortable. I think the point of it is to be worn for as short a time as possible. I was unsure of how to make a further move on my husband and was thankful when the phone rang and John answered it. It was our sons calling so as I was going to talk with them next, I got back up and went to John's side of the bed and stood—waiting. Hoping.

John handed me the phone and this time he did not take his eyes off me, thank God. When I hung up the phone, he put down his papers and responded as I had hoped. It was a truly wonderful night because I offered beauty—heart and soul and body.

Okay, my turn [John here]. This next story took place about two months ago, in the middle of the night.

When I awoke the clock said 2:30 A.M. I sensed Stasi tossing and turning next to me. We have had a lot of trouble with our sleep over the years, especially since we started Ransomed Heart Ministries. Most of it is spiritual attack. We've fought many long, hard battles for our sleep. Sometimes now I even dread bedtime, because it has been such a place of combat. A man gets tired of fighting after a while—especially when he doesn't always win. It can feel so emasculating. I'm the idiot; I can't get us protected here.

Anyhow, I was lying there awake, and I heard Stasi sigh. She did not know I was awake yet. I knew she needed me to intervene, to fight for her, to pray for her. But I was tired of all that. And if it did not work, it would be another defeat. I was feeling deeply ambivalent. Most men wait to move until victory is guaranteed. The moment of truth had come—I could just have rolled over, pretended to be asleep, and Stasi would never had known the difference.

I took a long deep breath, and let it out slowly. I did not want to be the wimp. So I rolled toward her and asked, "Honey, are you all right?" (Most men dread that question, because it opens the door into a realm they do not know what to do with. That is why asking the question is such a strong and loving thing to do.)

The backstory is that Stasi was hurting from some painful wounds delivered through a relationship with a friend. It was 2:30 in the morning and I just wanted to pray for her and try to go back to sleep, but I knew she needed to talk a bit. I could see the tears in her eyes in the moonlight. "Honey, what are you feeling?" I asked, and then I let her talk about it. We processed it together.

What we came to was some deep lies she believed about herself. Now a greater strength was called for. I began to gently but firmly tell her what is true. "These are the words of the enemy, sweetheart. This is *not* true about you. Stasi, you are trying to reason with a demon." It was abrupt, but she saw the lie for what it was. Up to this point I was tender. Now it was time for me to get fierce. I began to pray *over* her, against the evil one. (I was aware now of yet another choice—to offer strength, to sacrifice, because the more I intervened the more fully and totally awake I became, and my hope of sleep was now gone.) I brought the work of Christ against the lying spirits, the accusation, and the assault on our sleep. Several times over (this stuff is like felling a tree; it often takes a number of strong blows).

When I finished, I checked back in with Stasi. "How are you now?" "Much better." I sensed she was tender, and vulnerable. The moment cried out for a consummation. One more risk. What if she was not in a place for sex? What if it was the wrong call? It was 3:30 in the morning; maybe she just wanted to go back to sleep. I took her in my arms and initiated lovemaking, telling her all the while how beautiful she truly is.

A beautiful night, because I offered strength—heart, soul, and body.

All this is to say, ladies and gentlemen, that if it does not feel risky you are probably playing it safe. The riskiness adds fire to the passion.

And I can vouch that "rescue sex" is better even than "makeup sex."

Recovering Sexual Joy

The son of man came to seek and save what was lost.

——LUKE 19:10

The hopefulness of this promise is like a sunrise. Even as I read it again, having read it many times before, something in my heart quiets down a bit; the clamoring and the fear subside. God is about restoring the very things I care about, too. What a relief. We've got big help on our side. He knows something about resurrection.

We live in a love story set in the midst of a terrible war. So it should not come as a surprise that our sexuality is often a place of disappointment, sorrow, and loss. Maybe *the* place. The enemy specializes in wreaking havoc with human sexuality; when he wounds a man or woman here, he wounds them about as deeply as they can be wounded. Don't be surprised when your sexual intimacy is opposed; the sanctity of the marriage bed is a war zone. Before marriage, desire and passion don't seem to be a problem; well, keeping them in check is the problem. But often after the marriage vows the passion turns to fear, and the desire turns to hesitation. It is not just your marriage; it is everyone's. Because we are broken people with often very broken pasts, it can be hard to find consistent, abandoned sexual joy in marriage. But much can be recovered, and much can be healed.

And it is worth fighting for.

Now, there are many reasons for sexual difficulties, some far more serious than others. Treat this for the beautiful treasure it is; take it seriously. The help we offer here will take you a long way toward the recovery of deep, mutual sexual pleasure. But the things we speak to in this book may not be the reasons for your sexual struggles, and even if they are, understanding is not the same thing as healing; clarity does not always bring restoration. You might need professional help. Love your spouse enough to get it.

Okay, so how do you recover the sexuality of Eden? Heck, how 'bout just the sexuality of any town or village within a hundred miles of Eden? It begins by offering strength and beauty outside of the bedroom. The way you live and love in the everyday clears the path to your sexual bower, prepares your heart, and heals your love for one another so that you find yourself craving your spouse.

The next step can feel enormous—talk about it. Talk about your sexual life together. Ask your spouse how they are feeling about sex with you, what they enjoy, and what they would love to see happen. Most times I'm a little shy even to let Stasi see me naked and sexually aroused. For years we did not really talk about our sexuality. But it has been good to venture there and ask: "How was last night for you?" and, "What do you enjoy?" and even, "Can I tell you why I haven't seemed interested lately?"

Talking about your sexual life disarms speculation, the playground of the enemy. It also requires you to sort through your own feelings about your sexuality, which is a very good thing to do. Neglect leaves room for the cobwebs and spiders to move in. Your heart needs to be fully engaged here; if it's not, you want to know why not.

Then pray about it. Invite Christ into your sexuality, into your marriage bed. We *had* to do this for years, because so much of our past was hanging over the moment like dark clouds. At first we each prayed privately, not even knowing the other was praying; then we grew to the place where we could pray openly about it together. This has been absolutely incredible for us. Just this week I was feeling that there was too much distance between us, too much awkwardness. Stasi had been experiencing some physical discomfort when we made love; I let the enemy use it to accuse me. But I prayed that Jesus would come and restore our lovemaking, that he would fill it with his grace. Once again, he did.

Now, many of you were sexually active before marriage. Stasi and I both were, and it breaks my heart to say so. There is nothing glorious about it whatsoever, no matter what Hollywood might say. It does such damage. You have to deal with the past in order to take hold of your future. I was introduced to pornography in the third grade. Stasi was sexually abused when she was young; she was raped as a woman of twenty. Both of us experienced the sorrow of abortion. More than once. You have got to remember this love story is assaulted by evil. But if *we* can find our way—out of such pain, darkness, and sin—to a sexuality that is richer and better than ever before, then you can, too.

You *will* have to fight for healing and breakthrough; this does not just show up with the mail. The good news is, healing and breakthrough are available. Some of that we found through counseling; some we found through healing prayer. Some came as we fought the enemy, and some came simply as we chose to love one another. We have included a prayer for sexual healing in the back of this book; many people have found it very, very helpful. If you have a history of sexual activity outside of marriage, then you will want to pray through this prayer.

We know friends who have stopped having sex, either because of unresolved issues in their past or because of hard things in the present. We understand. We also think it is a really bad decision. God seems to think it is a really bad decision. The Scriptures allow for a time of separation; sometimes it's called for. But then God says,

> *The husband should fulfill his marital duty to his wife, and likewise the wife to her husband. The wife's body does not belong to her alone but also to her husband. In the same way, the husband's body does not belong to him alone but also to his wife. Do not deprive each other except by mutual consent and for a time, so that you might devote yourselves to prayer. Then come together again: . . .*

> (1 CORINTHIANS 7:3–5)

Do not give up sex unless you both agree ("by mutual consent") and only for short periods of time. None of this once-a-year-on-Valentine's-Day-sex-as-a-concession stuff. Now, of course, everyone's situation is deeply personal, and there are some relationships where sex has crossed the line into abuse. There is no justification for that.

The majority of marriages, at some point, hit sexual hard times. How do we love during them? Initiate anyway. Both of you. Even if you are afraid; even if you are not sure your spouse will respond. As a friend advised a young woman:

Sometimes you have to kiss in order to feel like kissing; sometimes you have to make love in order to feel like making love. When we submit to God's design for marriage whether we feel it or not, Jesus sets things into motion that we can never imagine or set into motion ourselves.

As a woman, I have the enormous joy of being in relationships with a few godly women who are older than I am. One afternoon, in the midst of a deep conversation, a wise woman told me that when her husband expresses a desire to be intimate, she never says no. *Never.* She had taken this Scripture to heart that her body is not hers alone anymore, but also her husband's. I had read similar advice in a book prior to getting married and I have tried to follow it as best I could. The thing is, women, as we all know, usually take longer to arouse sexually than men. The encouragement I was given was to respond to my husband's interest in a positive way, entrust myself to God, and love my man with my body, whether or not I felt like it in that moment. The result has only been good.

It might be helpful for you old-timers to get out of a rut. Change locations. Change positions. Turn on some music. Open a bottle of wine. Get away for the weekend to a nice hotel. Make out in the woods. Find out what it is that arouses your spouse and offer *that.*

"What I wish *he* knew . . ." Ladies, how would you fill in the rest of that? What I want to say to John is this—it is all about foreplay: The tone of your voice. The look in your eye. The gentle pat on the back as you pass by me. The way you cleared the table and dove in to help with the dishes. Your laughter. Sitting down next to me and asking me how I'm doing and what I have been thinking about. Reading aloud to me the part in the book that moved you. The tiny ways you convey that you enjoy me. Baby, that's it. My heart is yours. So now, in the bedroom, I'm all yours as well.

"What I wish *she* knew . . ." Men, what is it you wish your wife knew? What I want to say to Stasi is this: Where is that negligee? Wear it more often. I love it when you initiate. Wake me up in the night if you want to. I love it when you make me feel like the hero during the day, and when you say to me, "Honey, you are amazing." I want to know what pleases you. I want to know that *I* please you.

Drink Deeply

Our point is this—do not surrender this precious gift of God. Not until you are forced to by extreme old age or by some true physical malady.

A good marriage is a place where we are seen and loved, secure in the knowledge that our heart is being trusted as good, thought the best of, and even delighted in. And all that love, trust, and acceptance can find a resting place in the sanctuary of the marriage bed. Indeed our sexual intimacy is meant to be a place of sanctuary, a place of refuge and safety. Marriage is the relationship that provides the most hope for times of rest—a respite from the world of needing to prove ourselves—from having to work so hard to make ourselves understood and known. Instead, marriage is the place where we are meant to be able to "let down" and be our truest selves; to be known, loved, and welcomed. In that place, our souls and our bodies can rest into each other's loving embrace.

Good sex can be so healing for a marriage. Yes, it can mask other issues, but not for long. Sex can flush out what is going wrong in the marriage. You are not having sex. *Why* not? It has been a long time. *Why* is that? She doesn't have a desire, or he's not enjoying it. *Why?* Nine times out of ten, troubles in the bedroom are the flares going up because there are troubles elsewhere in the marriage. You would be a fool to ignore them.

Sexual intimacy in marriage is like fine wine. It gets better with time! Settling into the comfort and security of your spouse's love provides the best couch for intimate pleasure. It takes a while to really know each other. Trust grows over time. So does friendship. The ability to be honest about your sexuality increases as well.

It is just too easy to give way here, as with so many areas of life; it is too easy to resign yourself and surrender. Fight for a sexual life with your spouse that is frequent, and deeply satisfying for both of you. Take risks. Offer strength. Offer beauty. Be vulnerable. Be fully present. That is the way of love, *especially* in a time of war.

As God said, drink deeply, O lovers.

TWELVE

Learning to Love

Be imitators of God . . . and live a life of love.

——ST. PAUL

Some marriages make it, and some marriages don't: The odds are still running about 50/50.

The chances in favor of a *happy* marriage are even more slim, because as you well know simply the fact that a marriage has not fallen apart does not necessarily mean its members are thriving. Anybody can fake it for the Christmas photo. Many marriages "survive" by settling into soul-killing numbness, by using the distraction of busyness (as in raising children), or by tacitly agreeing to live separate lives while sharing the same roof. When rated on the marital bliss scale of 1 to 10, the majority of still-intact marriages hover around a 3, "Getting By." Some marriages carry on as violent, damaging maelstroms.

But there are couples who find their way to something beautiful. Truly beautiful.

We pray that you will be among them.

And we believe that if you will embrace the help offered here and stick with it for more than a couple of weeks—more than you stick with your diets, exercise, or savings plans—you have a much higher chance of joining those who have found their way to a beautiful and powerful marriage. But there is no guarantee, of course. You know that as well. So why bother? Why risk it? Why throw yourself wholeheartedly into such a dangerous, costly, and uncertain enterprise?

Measure your answer carefully.

"Because I know that he [or she] *will change"* is not a good answer. For you don't know that. If this is your reason you will forever take your cues from how your spouse is doing. You will become manipulative, and demanding. You will lose heart.

"Because God wanted us to get married, and so I know he will make it all work out." Maybe, but be careful what you claim God has promised you. Most of the Christian couples now divorced or living unhappily together thought God was in their union, too. That he has not seemed to rescue their marriage has shaken their faith like a rag doll.

"Because I promised to." This is closer to a very good answer. You did make your vows, after all. Taking those vows seriously will see you through years and years of hard times; they might even see you through to the end. Though many a good man and good woman find that those vows do not provide everything they need to remain fully *engaged* in their marriage. Being married to someone you know will never leave you and yet no longer truly loves you is not exactly what God had in mind.

We are not trying to be discouraging; we are trying to be realistic. This is a love story, set in the midst of war. Marriage is a crucible; the gladiatorial arena for love and war. It will eventually expose every broken place in you; it will reveal your every sin, if only before the watching heavens. Your commitment to self-protection will be confronted daily. You will be disappointed and you will be wounded. You will most certainly be *tested;* there may not be a greater test of character on the planet.

It begs the question—why in heaven's name would anyone throw themselves wholeheartedly into such a dangerous, costly, and uncertain enterprise?

"Because that is the kind of person I want to be."

Now that is a very good answer.

We Are Made for Love

I [John] have been reading a book written by a young soldier who fought through all four years of World War II. He saw the main action in Africa, Italy, Normandy, and Germany. A sensitive and thoughtful young man, he knew what terrible effects war has upon those who have to fight it. He opens the book with a letter he penned while at the front:

The last weeks have been hard, filled with many bitter, hateful things and only a few short happy interludes. Sometimes I feel very old. We have been a long time in the line. I have come to the extremity of knowing beyond all doubt that there is no other way for me to survive this period except the hard Christian way of finding the finer points in my associates and loving them for those characteristics. The bare, cold, prophetic words of Auden,

We must love one another or die

have rung in my mind on several of these frigid, sleepless nights of late.

Perhaps even you cannot participate enough in this life over here to understand. You would have to see a fine, fine family broken, people you had learned to love destroyed because of petty personal grudges. You would have to see people slapped and beaten because they might be telling a lie or because certain sadistic impulses need to be satisfied. You would have to see old men and women on the roads with a few pitiful belongings in a driving rain, going they know not where, trying to find shelter and a little food in a scorched-earth area. Oh, you would have to see many things to know why I should come to realize such a primitive truth as that I have only one alternative to death and that is to love.

(GLENN GRAY, *The Warriors*)

I found his letter bracing, like a plunge into a cold lake. Prophetic, too, honest truth from a life stripped of pretense. His thoughts came to me at a critical time. The past twelve months have been especially painful for us. Not, thank God, as a result of wounding each other, but through wounding in relationships very close to Stasi and me.

Things have been very hurtful. We have been a long time in the line, here in this love story set in the midst of war. The battle seems to be heating up, and the effects of living under the assault of evil takes its toll. Love seems foolish; it seems perfectly reasonable to hunker down and guard against further hurt.

Then I read the soldier's words, and I thought of Jesus' warning about the end of the age, how as times grow dark and people feel more keenly pressed, love will grow rare. "Nation will rise against nation, and kingdom against kingdom . . . Because of the increase of wickedness, the love of most will grow cold" (Matthew 24:7, 12). These are trying times, for all of us. I venture we will see even more trying times. But the soldier was right. Auden was right. We must love one another, or die.

Because love is what we are created for; it is the reason for our existence. Love is our destiny. Love God and love one another— these are the two great commands upon the human race. The secret to life is this—we are here in order to learn how to love.

It is really quite an epiphany when the truth finally strikes home. It might be the most liberating realization we ever come to. We are here in order to learn how to love. It is our greatest mission of all, our destiny.

Though it is the most basic of truths, this epiphany seems to come to few of us—or rather, it seems to be *accepted* by few of us. Most people remain committed to other things as their primary aim in life—happiness, survival, revenge, success, what have you. When a soul comes to accept the fact that they are here to learn how to love, that the course they have been enrolled in is "Learning to Love 101," it is as if the sun has just dawned for the first time in their life. All of these years they have lived underground and now they have just stepped out into the open air.

This was how I became a Christian.

I was nineteen at the time. My high school years were marked by the drug abuse and sexual license of the late sixties and early seventies. It left a hollow ache inside, and I began a spiritual search. Then Jesus just showed up one day. He really did. I can recall the evening. I was sitting in my bedroom, thinking about how desolate my life was. All my relationships were manipulative and dishonest; there was nothing true about them. My epiphany was simply this—I saw with utter clarity that I was not a loving person. I saw myself clearly, and what I saw was brutish, selfish, almost subhuman. I did not like what I was becoming.

To be unloving is to fail at the very thing we were created for. It is a rejection of the essence of our existence, a rejection of the Love that made us. As George MacDonald confessed, "I am a beast until I love as God doth love."

And so I turned to God that night, turned to him both for forgiveness, and for healing. I asked Jesus to heal my life, and help me become a loving man. That is how I became a disciple; I enrolled in his school of loving. I think you can fairly easily sort out the people who have come to this epiphany from those who have not. There is something different about their approach to life—what upsets them, what makes them laugh, and *especially* the way they handle people. These folks may not have named it, but a shift has taken place. It nearly always comes through a painful disruption of some sort. They discover that their style of relating is an absolute disaster; they might have lost someone dear to them. Sometimes it comes with illness, the shock that their days really are numbered and what will they live for now? The epiphany might arrive—as in my case—through a revelation of our own utter selfishness. It most often comes through some kind of encounter with God. He lives to love, and if you hang around Jesus long enough it rubs off on you.

However it may be delivered, the epiphany is the realization that life comes down to this, above all else: We are here to love.

This is the great shift, the most fundamental realignment of our heart's ambitions. It strikes at the very core of sin in us. It is not a dismal thing at all. Those who have made the shift are among the world's most joyful people. They are truly free.

I think of friends who have decided not to marry, and of those who are married but have decided not to have children. They are fundamentally selfish. There is just no other description for it. It isn't rocket science; they have figured out that life is easier when fewer people depend on you. I think about marriages we know, and the couples that aren't doing so well. Both parties seem truly stunned. It is more than disappointment; they seem completely taken by surprise. Their reaction betrays what they believe this Story is all about. "I'm not happy. You are not making me happy. When you do that you make me unhappy. In fact, you are making me miserable."

Now, we both understand the legitimate disappointments, and the very, very deep sorrow to be unhappy in your marriage. It is worse than being unhappy almost anywhere else in the world; even in prison or stranded on a desert island, because there you have some hope of release or of rescue. You hope for a way out. But in marriage, there is no way out but forward. As Mike Mason wrote in *The Mystery of Marriage,* "When the prison door of love clangs shut, the only thing to do is to become more in love than ever. There is just no other way to get out of it."

But still, the basic complaint reveals a fundamental flaw: you married in order to be happy. Didn't you? That is how God got you into it. Then he uses marriage to realign you to his purposes. Oh, there is happiness, gallons of it. I am embarrassed by how much happiness we've known. It is simply that the happiness awaits your realignment to the purposes of God.

No matter what you are told ahead of time about marriage, it does not matter one bit until you are *in* it, until you have lived *within* marriage for some time. Then you begin to understand. It's sort of like trying every key on a large ring of keys to see which one will open the Door to Life. The one labeled "My spouse will make me happy" doesn't seem to work. The pretty one called "Happy little home" doesn't work either. The gnarled one named "Protect yourself" doesn't fit. Well, I'll be doggone. There is only one key here that opens the door, and it's this one—"I am here to learn how to love." Huh. It is the last key most of us try.

But it opens the door all right, and then we can get on with actually living our lives.

A Thousand Little Choices

Don't you wish life had a soundtrack? It would be *so* helpful.

If some Alfred Hitchcock/Freddy Krueger creepy theme song began to play as I step into my house, I would be so much more ready to believe that spiritual warfare was real. If suddenly Josh Groban began singing in the background, I would know that romance was coming. If I tuned in to a tense, throbbing *Bourne Identity*–type theme song, I would know something dangerous was taking place. If it was time for me to be brave I would pick up my cue with panache if the theme song to *Gladiator* began to swell. Wouldn't it help you realize that you really do live in an epic if your life had a soundtrack?

Instead, all I hear right now is my neighbor's snowblower. It just does not have the same effect.

I think we all look for love to come in dramatic ways. We know love is powerful and beautiful. How come it doesn't *feel* like it? Love plays itself out in what seems like such unremarkable ways—you pick up your socks, you ignore her snarky comment, you put the toilet seat down. But this is exactly what makes it epic—the fact that love plays itself out in a thousand little choices, unseen and *without* supporting soundtrack. That is what makes it so beautiful.

A few years ago, John's parents reached their fiftieth wedding anniversary. To celebrate, we took them to Mexico for five days. The house we shared sat atop a hill overlooking the Sea of Cortez. Lounge chairs, hammocks, the sound of waves—it was gorgeous. But I'll tell you my favorite moment—the most beautiful sight that I was privileged to take in.

I don't know much about John's parents' marriage. I have a picture at home of a beautiful young woman laughing while sitting on the lap of a very happy young man. This was taken during their first year of married life. There was real love there. You could see it. But then the years piled up and life became hard. Things didn't go the way they dreamed or imagined. Their life was hard. Painful. John's dad's health has been steadily failing for many years. He is now forgetful. He can be impatient, sarcastic, crotchety—a real curmudgeon. But he has had one faithful companion who tends to him, pays attention to him, and cares for him—his wife.

Here was the moment. We were going out for a nice dinner this particular evening and Patricia had gotten herself ready. She is still a lovely woman and carries herself with style and grace. Bob was sitting in a chair, impatient to leave. "Not yet, Bob," she kindly said. And then she got down on her knees before him and helped him put on his new navy blue tennis shoes and carefully tied the laces. An ordinary, simple act that she has done for him hundreds, maybe thousands, of times. An act of such tender, unspoken, sacrificial love that it brought tears to my eyes.

Sometimes it is simply a touch. I [John] was feeling a little "bristly" this morning, like a pinecone with something to be resentful about, though I didn't know what it was. I simply was not feeling all that loving or lovable. Now, Stasi loves a hug in the morning; I know it brightens her day to be touched lovingly first thing when she comes out. But I did not feel like offering that. I was not in full retreat mode, just bristly. Before she came into the kitchen I turned my back to watch some deer out the window. All spines. Stasi came up from behind and lovingly touched me. What a beautiful choice on her part. The bristles fell away, like blowing on a dandelion.

This is difficult to write, because so many of these decisions are "secret" decisions, in that your spouse does not see them; these decisions are between each of us and God. So to write about them feels uncomfortable, like telling secrets. Letting your right hand know what your left hand is doing, or something like that. But we share a few in order to help you see how this might play out in your lives.

Our friends Craig and Lori were driving home to Colorado last weekend, returning from Los Angeles where they had spent the holidays with their children. They'd been gone for two weeks; it had been a lovely time. Now they were headed home. "I'm a stable horse," Craig confessed. "Turn me toward home and I just want to get back to the barn." Most guys can relate. Miles are something to be conquered; stopping is a form of surrender. (Especially when the semi you passed forty minutes ago lumbers past you while your wife lingers in the restroom.)

But Lori wanted to stop for lunch in Santa Fe. She loves cooking and Santa Fe has some wonderful cafés. It was also tantalizingly close to home, only five hours left of the eighteen-hour drive. Besides, their vacation was over. They had had a lot of nice meals in L.A. It was time to get home. Craig took Lori to lunch in Santa Fe; for two hours.

I'll run to the store.
We can watch your show.
Yes, you can dim the lights.
No, I don't mind if you go out tonight.
Would you like a little of my cookie?

We meet these moments every day. This morning, we had to get down to an event for which we were the keynote speakers. Stasi and I had agreed last night that we should leave the house at eight. It is now ten after eight and she is not ready; she is futzing in the bathroom. It's moments like these that reveal what fuels us. *Hey—you were the one who said eight. Let's go.* Why am I tweaked? What is with the compulsion, the anxiousness? Isn't it really about wanting to get on top of things, making sure we make a good impression? It is godless; I'm thinking about my reputation, not my wife's heart.

So, I sat at the kitchen table, finished my oatmeal, and had a cup of tea. I simply waited until she came out and said, "I'm ready." I didn't even get in that little dig men savor—"Finally." These are the little choices we are making every day. We are learning to love.

I'm Sorry

A happy marriage is the union of two forgivers.

—— RUTH BELL GRAHAM

I [Stasi] never wanted to be overweight. I did not wake up one day and say to myself, *I know what burden I'd like to bear—being seriously overweight! That will be my cross!* Nor did I ever long to have the pain of passing by a window or mirror and feeling utterly ashamed (many women know this shame). I hated that I was embarrassed of my body. Going out for a business dinner, meeting acquaintances of John's, speaking at an event—I felt I was an embarrassment to him and to the ministry God had given us.

Oh, I knew that other women were valuable regardless of their personal struggles or appearance. I understood that every *other* woman had something of incredible beauty to offer to the world. But I could not see that for myself. Every event, every outing, every vacation, every party, every gathering, every meeting, every single time I left the house I took with me my shame and embarrassment, my self-accusation and loathing. Why couldn't I just keep my mouth closed? Where was the spiritual discipline of *self*-discipline? My inability to lose weight and keep it off was hurting my husband terribly and even wounding my children.

Was it my fault? No. And yes. I did not want to be hurting them; I was *trying* to lose weight. Hard. My failure was all bound up in deep woundedness, spiritual strongholds, and sin. Did I intentionally wound my husband? Absolutely not. But I hurt him nonetheless. Did I—rather, *do I*—still need to ask his forgiveness for how I have wounded him? Yes, I think I do.

And this is hard for me to do. I want to place the blame on everyone else—"It's because of the wounds I received as a child." I want to blame the enemy—"It's all *his* fault!" Oh dear. I am sounding just like Eve. Lord have mercy.

I need to own up to my part. And I need to ask for my husband's forgiveness. I really do care more for his heart than I do for my own. Realizing that I have hurt him is painful. But I have to take the next step and apologize to him for it—specifically. I need to go to him in love and tell him that I see that I have hurt him, confess that I am deeply sorry, and ask for his forgiveness. Hurting my husband hardens his heart toward me. I lose his trust. Brick by brick a wall is slowly built up between us. Owning my part, acknowledging the pain I caused, repenting and asking for his forgiveness will hopefully bring that wall down.

Failing to love my husband well does not mean I am a failure. Hurting my husband does not mean I am a hurtful person. Sinning against him (or anyone else for that matter) does not mean my truest identity is as a sinner. As a child of God, I am holy and dearly loved. I am not a sinner but a saint. (And by the way, as a follower of Jesus Christ, you are, too.) I have a clean heart, a circumcised heart. My body is now the dwelling place, the temple of the living God. My identity is not up for grabs; it is settled. I belong to God and every single thing he says about me remains true. It is because of his amazing love and because I believe what he says about me, to me, that I am able to face my sin and failures and not turn into putty.

You just don't get through this broken, fallen, war-torn world without doing damage. A lot of the damage you don't even *know* you have done because it's coming from your own unconsidered style of relating. The cumulative effect of your sin and brokenness, and the cumulative effect of your approach to life over decades, dear friends, has had an effect on those around you. It is an effect you probably need to ask forgiveness for.

I [John] was asking Jesus the other day, "What do our readers need, Lord? What do their marriages need?"

He said, *Healing.*

So I asked, "How is the healing going to come?"

And he said, *Forgiveness.*

If there is to be an awakening of hope and desire, it is going to come through forgiveness. If there are to be some new frontiers in your relationship where you can talk about difficult things, handle conflicts differently, or approach sex differently, it is going to come through forgiveness.

We have done a lot of damage over the years.

All of us.

It will be the dawning of a new day and a very healing moment as we begin to ask forgiveness of one another. Simply sit down together and say, "I know what I need to ask forgiveness for" (if you do), or simply to ask, "What's it like to live with me? What has the effect of my style of relating been on you over the years? Has it caused you to lose hope in certain areas of our life? I really want to know and I really need your forgiveness." That would be so extraordinarily healing.

Now we know, we know, this sounds like jumping out of an airplane. Something in you is shouting: *There is no flippin' way. I'm not opening Pandora's box here—all those wounds, those issues we never really resolved. Are you crazy?*

We understand the fear. But dear friends, you can't ignore this. Eventually the buildup of all those offenses, great and small, shut a marriage down because our *hearts* shut down; part of us, anyway, shuts down, checks out, or catches a bus out of town. *It is never going to change and they don't seem all that concerned about their effect on me. I'm just not going to desire anymore, not going to have any hope.* You don't want your spouse coming to that conclusion. So you can't just blast past your impact on your spouse and hope for good things ahead.

Just as you can't in your relationship with God.

You know your intimacy with God is hurt by your sin, your indifference, your unbelief, your habitual addictions. In order to draw near to him, in order to recover the relationship, you have to say: "I'm sorry. Forgive me. I want to be close again, Lord Jesus. Come near to me. Forgive me for that outburst, that indulgence, for ignoring you for weeks. I really do love you." This is essential to the spiritual life. And you also know this is not a onetime thing. Our love with God is nurtured by forgiveness, healed by forgiveness, recovered through forgiveness over and over and over again.

Your spiritual life can't go anywhere without forgiveness. Marriage can't go anywhere without forgiveness.

We need to bring the healing grace of forgiveness into our marriages. What that looks like is sitting down together and putting something on the table: "Honey, I think maybe this [you will need to be specific] has been doing damage and I'm only now realizing it." Or asking your mate: "What's it like to live with me? What has the cumulative effect been upon you?" And if you are fortunate enough for your spouse to take the enormous risk of telling you, DO NOT do further damage by explaining it away or defending yourself: "Well, now hang on a second—you've got your issues, too," or "That is not what I meant at all—you took that totally wrong!"

Listen to what they have to say, acknowledge the weight of it, and then you say: "Sweetheart, I hear you. I am terribly sorry. Please, forgive me."

Timing is important. You want this to go well. When do you broach the subject? Talk to God about that. Pray beforehand. Pray hard.

And what *follows* is equally important. You don't want to sabotage the healing by repeating the very thing you did that caused you to ask for mercy in the first place. Your spouse needs to see real change; they need to see some conscious effort on your part or the enemy will be there in a flash with all the old agreements: *You see? Things will never change. Forget it. It's not worth it.*

Calm down. Take a deep breath. We know this sounds like a root canal without novocaine but God is with you. You are loved. You are forgiven. You are secure. You just have a little making up to do.

The Ultimate Reason

I'm sitting here writing this last chapter, blending Stasi's words with mine, two days before our deadline. Suddenly I'm aware— once again—that loving cuts right across the grain of my life.

I don't want to go ask forgiveness. I just want to get on with my day.

We have reached a peace accord; wouldn't it be better simply to let sleeping dogs lie? It certainly would be *easier,* and easy looks really attractive. The coward in me is having a fit. Once again I am so keenly aware that the way of love is going to require a different way of life for me. Man, this is costly. And dangerous. I hear the call, *Take up your cross,* coming to me from over the hills, as if from a distant land, another kingdom. Another choice to die to my self-protection, my self-centeredness, my way.

And so I find myself wrestling with the question we raised earlier: Why in heaven's name would anyone throw themselves *wholeheartedly* into such a dangerous, costly, and uncertain enterprise? (For wholehearted is the only way to live, and the only way love is really going to work; I do know that.)

My answer has changed over the years. Yes, this is the man I want to be; that is part of it. The integrity of living well is so restoring, so deeply satisfying to the soul, it is almost addicting. Yes, I take my vows seriously, even though I had no idea what I was saying when I first took them. But there is something deeper that calls to me, something richer I have tasted, which compels me to let go of the life I keep rebuilding in order to learn how to love.

I want God.

Can you name a better reason? There is simply no other fountain of life; there is no other waterfall of joy. God is the happiness we seek. This is what the Scriptures are trying to get across to us. Everyone who has known God and has written about it down through the ages agrees. But it is a truth you pay dearly to finally possess for yourself. "There is no other happiness than God," wrote Pascal, "and ourselves united to him." But boy oh boy is there happiness once you have God. David tasted friendship with God—after trying everything else—and came to the conclusion that "your love is better than life" (Psalm 63:3). Better even than life. Meaning, "I would give up my life in a heartbeat in exchange for the love of God."

Most people read words like this and they are not quite sure what to make of them. It's a difficult thing to identify with, if you haven't tasted for yourself how utterly good God is. It's like friends telling you about their trip to Switzerland, or Kauai. The more impassioned they get, the less it seems to help. All they can do is show you a few photos and urge you, "You really ought to go there and see for yourself."

The Christian life is like the chapel of San Vitale, in Ravenna. On the outside, the place is not that impressive; it could pass for a library. But inside it is absolutely breathtaking. Byzantine mosaics cover the walls, vaulted ceilings are inlaid with gold, arches upon arches, engraved marble floors. It is like stepping into another world, a fairy tale. They built it with the carpenter from Nazareth in mind. On the outside, he is not exactly your "American Idol." But inside he is the most engaging person you will ever meet. He will take your breath away.

I know this to be true, and I want more of him.

Now, to find God, I have to look where God is. This might help folks who report that God "seems distant," or as a friend recently commented (with a touch of cynicism), "he doesn't seem to come around much." If I want to find a hawk I look up in the sky, near the mountains where the thermals create an updraft. If I want to find our dog I simply have to find Stasi—he is usually curled up at her feet. Those who want to find God must look where he lives— must live in the same manner, for the same things, for the same reasons. "God is love. Whoever lives in love lives in God, and God in him" (1 John 4:16).

Every time we choose to love, we take a step closer to God; it is like he is right there. Every time we choose something else, we take a step away.

I want God, so I choose love.

Don't get me wrong; I love Stasi, more than ever. Sometimes it scares me how much I love her, because my heart feels so utterly out there, so entirely vulnerable. You step out that far and you know you are opening yourself up for hurt. "Love anything," C. S. Lewis says, "and your heart will be wrung and possibly broken." "Possibly" being an understatement. Then we read the Scriptures telling us to love one another "as God loved us," and if you had not made the connection yet that trail leads to a crown of thorns.

It does not come easy. Falling in love is how God gives us a push in the right direction. But then we have to choose. And we are going to need a very compelling reason to lay down our lives, day after day, year after year. To make those thousand little choices, for the thousand-and-oneth little time. Something needs to *compel* us.

What could be more compelling than this? When we abandon ourselves to love, we find ourselves closer to the one who is always doing that himself. We find God.

And then we discover a great surprise.

One of the mysteries of life runs like this. You do not find health by making health your aim. Nor do you find happiness by making happiness your aim. Nor does joy come to you because you go out looking for joy. You find all of those things only if you make something else your aim. When you find God you find all sorts of wonderful things. He made Eden, after all, and gave it to us like a wedding gift. The world is created for romance—music, vineyards, sunsets, a kiss. Drink deeply, lovers. That is the kind of person he is. He made our hearts, too, and gave us to one another. He wants joy and life for us, abundantly. "You open your hand and satisfy the desires of every living thing" (Psalm 145:16).

Like stepping inside the chapel of San Vitale, stepping into God I have found a dazzling life. I have a battle to fight now, as great as any man could ask for. I have adventure upon adventure. I have a stunning beauty to rescue (and you recall what happens after the rescue). Stasi has what every girl dreams of: she has someone to fight for her; she has a great adventure to share; she has more and more beauty to unveil. What joy passes from this partnering with God to see your spouse become more whole, and alive, and free?

Yes, loving costs everything. Look at the Cross. But loving is *always* worth it. John and I have been married over twenty-five years now and I can honestly tell you that it just gets better and better. I loved him with all my heart when I married him. But God has enlarged my heart as well as my love. It has cost me. It has cost John. It continues to. *But so does every great, priceless, beautiful treasure that is worth having.* I can't even begin to name all of the joys I have known through being married to John. They are the highest and the deepest of my life in God.

We live in a love story, set in the midst of war. Love is our destiny, and all hell is set against it. Really, it explains so much. We wake each morning and find that we have to fight our way back to all that is true; we have to fight off the thousands of reasons to settle for less than the life we were created for. Our bodies awaken but then our hearts and souls must awaken, too, so that we might play our part in the Grand Affair. And God has made our hearts in such a way that nothing awakens us quite like some great mission which is ours alone to fulfill. Thus the power of fairy tales, all of which turn on this awakening in the heart of the boy and the girl.

I expect this year will hold a number of battles. I imagine we will face down many demons together.

We will probably worry unnecessarily about our sons.

Despite our best intentions, I will leave my clothes piled on the floor and Stasi will tell me where to turn.

I am also looking forward to all of the joys that lie ahead. We laugh a lot these days.

I am hoping we make it back to the Tetons, and maybe even get to Italy.

EPILOGUE

What Now?

You made it through the book—congratulations!

Now what?

Stasi and I would like to offer a few "next steps":

Read the book again! I just finished reading the entire book again, months after Stasi and I first wrote it. What a surprise! I found myself struck by things that didn't strike me the first time, reminded of truths I completely forgot, deeply encouraged, somewhat convicted, and *moved* to make our marriage better. I think that you will find the same—that this takes more than one reading!

Give a copy to your spouse (or fiancé) and ask them to read it! Then set a few evenings aside to talk about it. Better still, make it a weekend away, do something romantic and talk about the book—what moved you, what you'd love to work through in your marriage. It might be a good time to talk about your dreams and desires; it might be the time to ask forgiveness of one another.

Invite a few couples you know to get together and do a "book group." Go through it together. Talk about it. You'll find the *Love & War* DVD series perfect for your group to use! We've done this several times, and it has been one of the best investments we've ever made in our marriage!

Give *Love & War* to couples whose marriages you want to encourage, even rescue!

Come to www.loveandwar.net to find out more about our marriage events, retreats for men and women, podcasts, and a whole host of other resources to help you find the life God has for you, your spouse, and your marriage! There is *more*!

Prayers

A Prayer to Receive Jesus Christ as Savior

Jesus, I believe you are the Son of God, that you died on the Cross to rescue me from sin and death and to restore me to the Father. I choose now to turn from my sins, my self-centeredness and every part of my life that does not please you. I choose you. I receive your forgiveness and ask you to take your rightful place in my life as my Savior and Lord. Come reign in my heart, fill me with your love and your life, and help me to become a person who is truly loving—a person like you. Restore me, Jesus. Live in me. Love through me. Thank you, God. In Jesus' name I pray. Amen.

Daily Prayer

Over the years Stasi and I have grown more and more appreciative of the benefits of daily prayer—both as individuals and as a couple. It has been a journey. When we were starting out, we found great help through simple prayers such as,

> *Lord Jesus we give you our home, our marriage, and our family.*
> *Cover us with your blood and fill us with your life. Come and be the*
> *Lord of our marriage and home and family.*

Over time we found we needed to pray a bit more. Part of this comes as the battles increase; part of it is the natural process of growing in our spiritual lives. We offer here the "Daily Prayer" that we and the folks at our ministry, Ransomed Heart, pray each day. Yes, it can seem a little lengthy, but over time you will find enormous spiritual protection and joy by praying this or something like it on a regular basis. (This is actually a shorter version than the one we now pray!)

Now, most days Stasi and I run on a different morning schedule and so we pray this prayer individually, but in the spirit of "standing together" knowing the other is also praying and "agreeing together" in prayer. Other times we find we need to pray together at the same time, in the same room, because the need for united prayer has become pressing. Either way, this has been an enormous blessing to us.

> *My dear Lord Jesus, I come to you now to be restored in you, to be*
> *renewed in you, to receive your love, your life, and all the grace and*
> *mercy I so desperately need this day. I honor you as my Sovereign*
> *Lord, and I surrender every aspect of my life totally and completely to*
> *you. I give you my spirit, soul, and body, my heart, mind, and will. I*
> *cover myself with your blood—my spirit, soul, and body, my heart,*
> *mind, and will. I ask your Holy Spirit to restore me in you, renew me*

in you, and lead me in this time of prayer. In all that I now pray, I stand in total agreement with your Spirit, and with {my spouse, by name}.

{Now, if you are a husband, you'll want to include your wife in this time of prayer. If you are a parent, you'll want to include your children.}

In all that I now pray, I include {my wife and/or children, by name}. Acting as their head, I bring them under your authority and covering, as I come under your authority and covering. I cover {wife and/or children, by name} with your blood—their spirit, soul, and body, their heart, mind, and will. I ask your Spirit to restore them in you, renew them in you, and apply to them all that I now pray on their behalf, acting as their head.

Dear God, holy and victorious Trinity, you alone are worthy of all my worship, my heart's devotion, all my praise, all my trust and all the glory of my life. I love you, I worship you, I trust you. I give myself over to you in my heart's search for life. You alone are Life, and you have become my life. I renounce all other gods, all idols, and I give you the place in my heart and in my life that you truly deserve. I confess here and now that this is all about you, God, and not about me. You are the Hero of this story, and I belong to you. Forgive me for my every sin. Search me and know me and reveal to me where you are working in my life, and grant to me the grace of your healing, deliverance, and a deep and true repentance.

Heavenly Father, thank you for loving me and choosing me before you made the world. You are my true Father—my Creator, Redeemer, Sustainer, and the true end of all things, including my life. I love you, I trust you, I worship you. I give myself over to you to be one with you in all things, as Jesus is one with you. Thank you for proving your love by sending Jesus. I receive him and all his life and all his work, which you ordained for me. Thank you for including me in Christ, for forgiving me my sins, for granting me

*his righteousness, for making me complete in him. Thank you for
making me alive with Christ, raising me with him, seating me
with him at your right hand, establishing me in his authority, and
anointing me with your Holy Spirit, your love, and your favor. I
receive it all with thanks and give it total claim to my life—my
spirit, soul, and body, my heart, mind, and will. I bring the life
and the work of Jesus over {wife and/or children, by name} and
over my home, my household, my vehicles, finances, all my kingdom
and domain.*

*Jesus, thank you for coming to ransom me with your own life. I love
you, I worship you, I trust you. I give myself over to you, to be one
with you in all things. And I receive all the work and all of the
triumph of your Cross, death, blood, and sacrifice for me, through
which I am atoned for, I am ransomed and transferred to your
kingdom, my sin nature is removed, my heart is circumcised unto God,
and every claim made against me is disarmed this day. I now take my
place in your Cross and death, through which I have died with you to
sin, to my flesh, to the world, and to the evil one. I take up the Cross
and crucify my flesh with all its pride, arrogance, unbelief, and
idolatry {include anything else you are currently struggling with}. I
put off the old man. I ask you to apply to me the fullness of your Cross,
death, blood, and sacrifice. I receive it with thanks and give it total
claim to my spirit, soul and body, my heart, mind, and will.*

*Jesus, I also sincerely receive you as my life, my holiness, and strength,
and I receive all the work and triumph of your resurrection, through
which you have conquered sin and death and judgment. Death has no
mastery over you, nor does any foul thing. And I have been raised
with you to a new life, to live your life—dead to sin and alive to
God. I now take my place in your resurrection and in your life,
through which I am saved by your life. I reign in life through your
life. I receive your life—your humility, love and forgiveness, your
integrity, your wisdom, strength, joy, your union with the Father.
Apply to me the fullness of your resurrection. I receive it with thanks*

and give it total claim to my spirit, soul and body, my heart, mind, and will.

Jesus, I also sincerely receive you as my authority, rule, and dominion, my everlasting victory against Satan and his kingdom, and my ability to bring your kingdom at all times and in every way. I receive all the work and triumph of your ascension, through which you have judged Satan and cast him down, you have disarmed his kingdom. All authority in heaven and on earth has been given to you, Jesus. I now take my place in your ascension, and your throne, through which I have been raised with you to the right hand of the Father and established in your authority. I now bring the Kingdom of God and the authority, rule, and dominion of Jesus Christ over my life today, over my home, my household, my vehicles and finances, over all my kingdom and domain.

I now bring the authority, rule, and dominion of the Lord Jesus Christ, and the fullness of the work of Christ, against Satan, against his kingdom, against every foul and unclean spirit that is against me. {At this point you might want to name the specific battles and enemies you know have been attacking you.} I bring the full work of Jesus Christ against every foul power and black art. I bind it all from me in the authority of the Lord Jesus Christ and in his Name. I also keep the Cross of Jesus Christ between me and all people, so that only the love of Christ may pass between us.

Holy Spirit, thank you for coming. I love you, I worship you, I trust you. I sincerely receive you and all the work and victory in Pentecost, through which you have come, you have clothed me with power from on high, sealed me in Christ. You have become my union with the Father and the Son, become the Spirit of truth in me, the life of God in me, my Counselor, Comforter, Strength, and Guide. I honor you as my Sovereign, and I yield every dimension of my life to you and you alone, to be filled with you, to walk in step with you in all things. Fill me afresh. Restore my union with the Father and the Son. Lead me in all truth, anoint me for all of my life and walk and calling, and lead me deeper into Jesus today. I receive you with thanks, and I give you total claim to my life. Heavenly Father, thank you for granting to me every spiritual blessing in Christ Jesus. I claim the riches in Christ Jesus over my life today. I bring the blood of Christ over my spirit, soul, and body, my heart, mind, and will. I put on the full armor of God—the belt of truth, breastplate of righteousness, shoes of the gospel, helmet of salvation. I take up the shield of faith and sword of the Spirit, and I choose to wield these weapons at all times in the power of God. I choose to pray at all times in the Spirit.

Thank you for your angels. I ask for their help and protection this day, ask that they establish your kingdom through my kingdom and domain. I now call forth the kingdom of the Lord Jesus Christ throughout my home, my family, my kingdom, and my domain, in the authority of the Lord Jesus Christ, with all glory and honor and thanks to him.

A Prayer for Sexual Healing

Healing for your sexuality is available; this is a very hopeful truth! But you must realize that your sexuality is very deep and core to your nature as a human being. Sexual brokenness can be one of the deepest types of brokenness a person can experience. You must take your healing and restoration seriously. This guided prayer will help immensely. You may find you need to pray through it a few times in order to experience a lasting freedom.

A bit of explanation on the reasons for the prayer: First, when we misuse our sexuality through sin we give Satan an open door to oppress us in our sexuality. A man who uses pornography will find himself in a very deep struggle with lust; a woman who was sexually promiscuous before marriage may find herself wresting with sexual temptation years afterward. So it is important to bring our sexuality under the Lordship (and therefore protection) of the Lord Jesus Christ and seek his cleansing of our sexual sins. Second, sexual brokenness—whether through abuse of our sexuality by our own actions or by the actions of others—can create sexual difficulties, and also opens the door for the enemy to oppress us. Quite often forgiveness is needed—both the confidence that we are forgiven by the Lord and the choice we make to forgive others. This will prove immensely freeing.

Let us begin by bringing our lives and sexuality under the Lordship of Jesus Christ:

Lord Jesus Christ, I confess here and now that you are my Creator (John 1:3) and therefore the creator of my sexuality. I confess that you are also my Savior, that you have ransomed me with your blood (1 Corinthians 15:3, Matthew 20:28). I have been bought with the blood of Jesus Christ; my life and my body belong to God (1 Corinthians 6:19–20). Jesus, I present myself to you now to be made whole and holy in every way, including in my sexuality. You ask us to present our bodies to you as living sacrifices (Romans 12:1) and the

*parts of our bodies as instruments of righteousness (Romans 6:13). I
do this now. I present my body, my sexuality {"as a man" or "as a
woman"} and I present my sexual nature to you.*

Next you need to renounce the ways you have misused your sexuality. The more specific you can be the more helpful this will be.
Your sexuality was created by God for pleasure and joy within the
context of the marriage covenant. Sexual activity outside of marriage can be very damaging to a person and to their relationships (1
Corinthians 6:18–20). What you want to do in this part of the
prayer is confess and renounce all sexual sin—for example, sexual
intimacy outside of marriage. Not only intercourse, but other
forms of sexual intimacy such as mutual masturbation or oral sex.
Many people assume these "don't really count as sin" because they
didn't result in actual intercourse; however, there was sexual stim-
ulation and intimacy outside marriage. Keep in mind there is the
"Spirit of the law" and the "letter of the law." What matters are issues of heart and mind as well as body. Other examples of sins to renounce would be extramarital affairs, the use of pornography, and
sexual fantasies.

You may know exactly what you need to confess and renounce; you
may need to ask God's help to remember. Take your time here. As
memories and events come to mind, confess and renounce them. For
example: "Lord Jesus I ask your forgiveness for my sins of masturbation and using pornography. I renounce those sins in your name."
After you have confessed your sins—and don't get tied up trying to
remember each and every one, just trust God to remind you—then go
on with the rest of the prayer.

*Jesus, I ask your Holy Spirit to help me now remember, confess and
renounce my sexual sins. {Pause. Listen. Remember. Confess and
renounce.} Lord Jesus, I ask your forgiveness for every act of sexual
sin. You promised that if we confess our sins you are faithful and just
to forgive us our sins and cleanse us from all unrighteousness (1 John*

1:9). I ask you to cleanse me of my sexual sins now, cleanse my body, soul, and spirit, cleanse my heart and mind and will, cleanse my sexuality. Thank you for forgiving me and cleansing me. I receive your forgiveness and cleansing. I renounce every claim I have given Satan to my life or sexuality through my sexual sins. Those claims are now broken by the Cross and blood of Jesus Christ (Colossians 2:13–15).

Next comes issues of forgiveness. It is vital that you forgive both yourself and those who have harmed you sexually. LISTEN CAREFULLY: Forgiveness is a *choice;* we often have to make the *decision* to forgive long before we *feel* forgiving. We realize this can be difficult, but the freedom you will find will be worth it! Forgiveness is not saying, "It didn't hurt me." Forgiveness is not saying, "It didn't matter." Forgiveness is the act whereby we pardon the person, we release them from all bitterness and judgment. We give them to God to deal with.

Lord Jesus, I thank you for offering me total and complete forgiveness. I receive that forgiveness now. I choose to forgive myself for all of my sexual wrongdoing. I also choose to forgive those who have harmed me sexually. {Be specific here; name those people, and forgive them.} I release them to you. I release all my anger and judgment toward them. Come Lord Jesus, into the pain they caused me, and heal me with your love.

This next step involves breaking the unhealthy emotional and spiritual bonds formed with other people through sexual sin. One of the reasons the Bible takes sexual sin so seriously is because of the damage it does. Another reason is because of the bonds it forms with people, bonds meant to be formed only between husband and wife (see 1 Corinthians 6:15–20). One of the marvelous effects of the Cross of our Lord Jesus Christ is that it breaks these unhealthy bonds. "May I never boast except in the Cross of our Lord Jesus

Christ, through which the world has been crucified to me and I to the world" (Galatians 6:14).

> *I now bring the Cross of my Lord Jesus Christ between me and every person with whom I have been sexually intimate. {Name them specifically whenever possible. Also, name those who have abused you sexually.} I break all sexual, emotional, and spiritual bonds with {name if possible, or just "that girl in high school" if you can't remember her name}. I keep the Cross of Christ between us.*

Many people experience negative consequences through the misuse of their sexuality. Those consequences might be lingering guilt (even after confession) or repeated sexual temptation. Consequences might also be the inability to enjoy sex with their spouse. It will help to bring the work of Christ here as well. Many people end up making unhealthy "agreements" about sex or themselves, about men or women or intimacy, because of the damage they have experienced through sexual sin (their sin, or the sin of someone against them). You will want to ask Christ what those agreements are, and *break them!*

> *I renounce {name what the struggle is—"the inability to have an orgasm" or "this lingering shame" or "the hatred of my body"}. I bring the Cross and blood of Jesus Christ against this {guilt or shame, every negative consequence}. Lord Jesus, I also ask you to reveal to me any agreements I have made about my sexuality or this specific struggle. {An example would be "I will always struggle with this" or "I don't deserve to enjoy sex now" or "My sexuality is dirty." Pause and let Jesus reveal those agreements to you. Then break them.} I break this agreement {name it} in the name of my Lord Jesus Christ, and I renounce every claim I have given it in my life.*

Finally, it will prove helpful to consecrate your sexuality to Jesus Christ once more.

Lord Jesus, I now consecrate my sexuality to you in every way. I consecrate my sexual intimacy with my spouse to you. I ask you to cleanse and heal my sexuality and our sexual intimacy in every way. I ask your healing grace to come and free me from all consequences of sexual sin. I ask you to fill my sexuality with your healing love and goodness. Restore my sexuality in wholeness. Let me and my spouse both experience all of the intimacy and pleasure you intended a man and woman to enjoy in marriage. I pray all of this in the name of Jesus Christ my Lord. Amen!!

We could report many, many stories of stunning redemption that have come as a result of individuals and couples praying through this type of prayer. Now remember—sometimes the wounds and consequences take time to heal. You might want to revisit this prayer several times over if lasting healing has not yet taken place. You may recall actions that need confession long after you finish this book; return to this prayer, and confess those as well. Some of you will also benefit from seeing a good Christian counselor. Hold fast to these truths:

You, your body, and your sexuality belong to Jesus Christ.
He has completely forgiven you.
He created your sexuality to be whole and holy.
He created your sexuality to be a source of intimacy and joy.

Jesus Christ came to seek and save "what was lost" (Luke 19:10), including all that was lost in the blessings he intended through our sexuality!

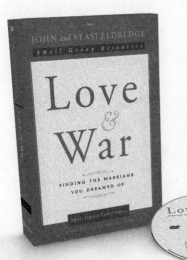

DISCOVER A WHOLE TREASURE CHEST AT RANSOMED HEART!

John and Stasi, and their team at Ransomed Heart Ministries, offer a wealth of exciting and life-changing resources through their ministry…

- **Marriage Conferences**
- **Retreats for Men and Women**
- **Audio and Video resources**
- **Daily encouragement through blogs, podcasts, daily readings**
- **Group and Individual study kits**
- **Online community and forums**

We want you to know *there is so much more!* Come and connect with us!

www.RansomedHeart.com/LWsignup

Dive in today by signing up for email encouragement, and exploring our resources and events — created to help you find the life God intended for you.

Receive

30% off*
any one item,
as our way of welcoming you.

For a limited time, sign-up to be eligible to

WIN a FREE
ALL EXPENSE
PAID TRIP*
to a men's or women's event

*See details online at www.ransomedheart.com/LWsignup